RAISING CHILDREN THE BIBLE WAY

and the

CHRISTIAN ASSERTIVE EFFORT

RAISING CHILDREN THE BIBLE WAY

and the

CHRISTIAN ASSERTIVE EFFORT

WILLIAM R. SCOTT

Pleasant Word
A Division of WINEPRESS PUBLISHING

Printed in the United States of America

Packaged by Pleasant Word, a division of WinePress Publishing, PO Box 428, Enumclaw, WA 98022. The views expressed or implied in this work do not necessarily reflect those of Pleasant Word, a division of WinePress Publishing. Ultimate design, content, and editorial accuracy of this work are the responsibilities of the author.

Unless otherwise noted, all Scriptures are taken from the Holy Bible, New International Version, Copyright © 1973, 1978, 1984 by the International Bible Society. Used by permission of Zondervan Publishing House. The "NIV" and "New International Version" trademarks are registered in the United States Patent and Trademark Office by International Bible Society.

Scripture references marked KJV are taken from the King James Version of the Bible.

Scripture references marked NASB are taken from the New American Standard Bible, © 1960, 1963, 1968, 1971, 1972, 1973, 1975, 1977 by The Lockman Foundation. Used by permission.

ISBN 1-4141-0000-0
Library of Congress Catalog Card Number: 2003107643

Table of Contents

Introduction

The importance of the Gospel Model, and the terminology that defines the Gospel Model, is that it opens the door to a new discussion of Christ. The enlightened use of the Gospel Model provides a new area of discussion for the modern day church while preserving all the traditional values that the church of Jesus Christ is not willing to forsake.

Christ interpreted as a model of behavior places Christianity into the center of the forums of science, philosophy, socialization, and education. These form the main matrix of society and are the paths through which the American culture grows. Humanism has advanced its presence into the American culture through all these avenues. Christianity, in taking its message to society, must enlarge its initiative in order to make Jesus Christ more acceptable than a humanistic approach. The new definition of Christ allows fundamental Christianity to speak to both the church and the world to explain the Christian effort and initiative. It is as much of an epiphany from God to Christianity as was the revelation of Martin Luther that the "just shall live by faith." The definition of the Gospel Model is that important.

Christianity has been late in its response to the liberalism of humanism. Liberal social designers who desire to leave Christianity out of the equation of social design have labeled the church as an institution in decline. The Gospel Model offers an approach to the church that will quicken its influence back into the matrix of society. The Gospel Model, like God Himself, offers the world a dynamic and action-designed model that encompasses and promotes the infusion of fundamental Christianity strongly into the culture.

Christianity can not accept the premise of humanism that says God can not be part of the human and political formation of culture. To become firmly planted in both the heart of children and society is the main thrust and purpose of the Gospel Model. This effort, called *the Christian Assertive Effort* speaks clearly to humanism as an antithesis to gloom, doom, and failure. Our Bible teaches that we are what we do, that Christianity is to overcome humanism, and that we can fulfill the goal of taking the Gospel Model to society.

As the Gospel Model, Christ expects the church to involve Him in every effort made by the church. If the church fails to be infused by the Gospel Model, the expectation that the world will receive Christ is hopeless. Therefore, the main purpose of the book *Raising Children the Bible Way* and the *Christian Assertive Effort* is to delineate exactly what Christ the Gospel Model is and define the model so Christ can be used efficiently in all Christian endeavors.

Chapter One

Good News

COMMUNITY CHURCH COMES ALIVE! REACHES OUT TO AT-RISK CHILDREN AND ADOLESCENTS

Peculiar Behavior Of Rev. Doe

The Rev. John Doe made a discovery about himself. He had inadvertently learned spiritual helplessness. He was powerless to influence the community and to involve his church in important community issues. The harder he worked the more he felt isolated from the community.

Rev. Doe was a speaker and hearer, but not a doer of the word. His well-packaged services to the community seemed empty. This feeling helped him to realize what being a doer of the word was. Doing the word was actually sowing seed in soil that he had cultivated and tilled. He began to see the formula that God had for building the kingdom of God as expressed in the image of Jesus Christ, which he called the Gospel Model of behavior.

Jesus as a behavioral model was new information. God's model of Christian behavior was to be used to guide parents in raising children, and churches in reaching out to the community. The Gospel Model was quickly to become a guide to school principals and teachers, psychologist, doctors, counselors, social workers, and church committees. The new vision of Rev. Doe was changing the community.

Rev. Doe used the Gospel Model in all parts of his life. He set goals for self-improvement, physical fitness, and professional preparedness. The Gospel Model was an epiphany, an awakening that had excited and prepared many persons to share the gospel with others. The new model was especially rewarding to people who had not previously found a way to share the gospel.

He began with Mrs. Doe who was a schoolteacher. She used the Gospel Model in lesson plans and setting educational goals for her students. It was remarkable! Students who normally misbehaved became model students. The slow-learning children began to catch up with and sometimes passed the best students in her class. Mrs. Doe became so excited that she shared the Gospel Model of behavior with other teachers. The guidance counselor became very interested due to the effect it visibly had on student behavior. The seed sown by Rev. Doe multiplied many times throughout the school and community.

Rev. Doe began to train all Christians in the Gospel Model. Once a member caught on to using the model, the new knowledge became contagious The Holy Spirit was evidently involved. All efforts in the church became organized on the basis of the Gospel Model.

The church worked with children that were socially and emotionally at risk. Church members formed clubs and committees dedicated to *doing the word* type of things and joined the pastor in his assertive effort to reach out to at-risk children.

The church began a program to train parents on how to raise children the Bible way. People who had previously rejected attending church as a solution to their problems became interested in hearing about the new thinking of Rev. Doe. His sermons became interesting as he explained something new to a needy community. The church took on an inquisitive attitude, one of learning and doing.

The school principal, Mr. W. R. Pal, who attended Rev. Doe's church, instructed his teachers to follow a specific model of behavior while teaching students. He provided reading materials about models that paralleled the Gospel Model. Teachers adhered to three simple rules, which made up how they were to teach. The new rules energized their teaching. The way they taught became more productive.

Step one, teachers adopted high behavioral and learning goals for themselves and each student. Students accepted the goals as their own. The goals were both short and long term. Mary wanted to learn to read and Johnny wanted to be a doctor. Step two, the teachers and students identified what each would have to do for Mary to learn to read and Johnny to be a doctor. Step three, the students and teachers associated *what they were* with *what they did*. Girls were beautiful because they acted with beauty and grace and ball players were good because they practiced the needed skills. Teachers associated high-test scores of students as a sign of good teaching. Mr. Pal was praised in the local newspaper for his school's work with students at risk and won several statewide awards. Teachers and students were under the influence of the Gospel Model, although not a word of religion had been mentioned.

People who moved into the community placed their children in Mr. Pal's school with genuine expectations for success. This school had a certain peculiarity about it. It was no surprise that the newcomers to the community attended Rev. Doe's church.

Among the churches in the community, this church was very peculiar also. The religious community said that Rev. John Doe's church was having a revival.

The church initiated a building program to accommodate a new attendance of church members. Members of the church developed skills of counseling and child rearing. As a lay person in the church, Mr. Pal worked with parents, children, and adolescents who needed the Gospel Model. The model provided knowledge in a self-perpetuating manner. The church outlined for parents the way to raise children according to behavioral principles found in the Bible.

New Interpretations

Rev. Doe knew Christ was the model of behavior that made him successful. He was no longer a helpless Christian. Church members also learned they were not following correctly following God as Christ was never non-responsive to the spiritual needs of the community. For example, when the local school district outlawed praying at all school events, members of John Doe's church only mumbled and then acquiesced to the New Age standard. It was too politically incorrect for them to protest the loss of another Christian stronghold for fear of being called the religious right. Nothing stirred about this issue and no Christian protest was made. The Rev. John Doe concluded that he and his church were not really following the model of Christ but a different life style that resembled a humanistic model that was none religious.

There was a great need to correct the understanding the church and community had of the Word of God. It was his job to make the Word more meaningful in modern day religion. Rev. Doe discovered that God was a *verb*. God had told Moses, "I am" that I am. God was whatever He did. God asked Rev. Doe to follow the same pattern of behavior that God Himself followed.

Rev. Doe encouraged parents to actively raise children by following a life style promoted by the Gospel Model. Engage the needy was his new theme. Christ went to the crippled and dying to perform great miracles on them. The church does greater and more spiritual miracles today when it actively engages society to the saving and protecting of children from at-risk factors. God blesses parents to make them adaptive and able to lead children to success, which is a miracle. The church must keep dominion over the offspring of Adam and raise children in God's wonderful plan for success.

What the Church Needs Now

Several times God wiped away the past to provide mankind a second chance. In Noah's day the Flood created an opportunity for parents to begin anew. The only ones preserved from the Flood were the children of Noah and their wives. God blessed them and told them to replenish the earth. The blessing in the Bible was the ability to raise children and God wants us to remember this fact.

In Moses' day the children of God had forgotten what a redeemer the Lord God Almighty was. They really found it difficult to believe that Moses could deliver them, although they continually prayed for deliverance. A humanist called Pharaoh had taken control of the people's minds. The community or church today can also be taken over by humanism, which means the people have forgotten again what the Almighty can do.

The church and parents are to provide the admonition and nurture that Moses provided the Hebrew children. Before Moses, the Hebrew children had leaders who were too ineffective, much like Rev. Doe had been. The old leaders became jealous of Moses. Quickly, Moses found out that not all leaders in God's family really wanted salvation for everybody. The old leaders caused the Hebrew children to want to turn away from

God to return to Egypt, but God swallowed into the ground the leaders who allowed Israel to backslide. God made a covenant or agreement with Israel through the laws of Moses, an agreement that Israel would always be blessed, providing Israel kept the agreement. Moses re-trained the mothers, fathers, and elders to the new laws of God. Moses trained parents by harsh and very exact laws, because the Hebrew children needed a comprehensive law that covered all areas of living. The blessing—the ability to raise children—was worth the struggle of learning a new lifestyle. It was a new beginning.

When Jesus Christ came into the world, the children of God were beaten down again and discouraged. They needed a new beginning. The appearing of Christ was a great event. God the Father was making the maximum effort to show Israel the way. The twelve apostles presented Christ Himself to society. Christ appearing or His revelation appears to each generation so that all future generations can have a new blessing.

The Gospel Model is Christ. The power for performance comes from Jesus. He provides a steady stream of power that can light up the whole world. The plan has always been for you to take the good news to the world.

Jesus Christ taught that He was the model of God. Here is the formula that Moses' God Himself followed. "What I am" = "What I do" = "What I did I am." In the Bible there is only one plan for raising children and saving souls. There are only Christians "in action" making maximum efforts. It is the Gospel Model that makes all programs work effectively. Programs are good if God is in the programs.

Something New in the Community

Something strange occurred. Delegates representing the churches and parent teacher organizations made appearances together for the first time at the county school board meeting.

The delegates were not demanding or hostile as previous delegations had been. This group wanted to help the school board to write policies and regulations that were representative of the values of the community.

The group said they were making a *Christian Assertive Effort to* identify what policies and regulations the school board had adopted that were in harmony with the values of the community. The community believed in creationism and an absolute God as detailed in the Constitution of the United States. If the school board felt restraint in allowing Christian activities in schools, then the accommodations paid to the humanist philosophy must also be disallowed. Too many Christians were being offended by the intrusion of humanism. The school board did not know how to respond or how to answer the *Christian Assertive Effort* delegation. The delegation agreed to serve on a committee to help the school board re-write its philosophy of education. The school board had not really realized it had adopted so many humanistic policies.

In the book of Acts, Christians are challenged to spread the Christian religion throughout society. St. Paul and the apostles encouraged Christians to study to be able to answer the criticisms of those who would steal away the hope of the believers. The Rev. John Doe had stirred up his congregation and community to a learning frenzy. They continued to learn a new definition of a Christian practicing his religion.

Christian education became defined as putting the Gospel Model to work in the lives of children and adults. Christian teachers were doing this in both public and private schools. Parents learned how to control the learning process in schools in order to provide a Christian education for students. Christian influence limited the use of humanistic rules and policies by practicing policies Christians made.

How to Begin a Christian Assertive Effort

After Christ's resurrection the disciples were to take the Gospel Model into all of society. That must be the starting point for any real effort made for Christ. The church was given a plan to impact education, politics, businesses, and the human condition. The plan was used in fulfilling the Great Commission: *Go ye into all the world, and preach the gospel to every creature* (St. Mark 16:15).

The world is society, not a geographic location. God wants society to be Christian, so society will automatically respond to life events in a way that glorifies God. This automatic response was seen in World War II when American and Allied forces stopped humanistic Nazism. Directly thereafter the words of *under God* was placed into the pledge to the flag of the United States.

The church needs to rediscover ways to plant the Word into society. We must not allow Satan to gain ground and strongholds. In St. Matthew 28:19–20, Jesus commands His disciples to teach all nations (societies) the things that He commanded and that, if this were done, God would be with them. Society cannot be taught from inside the walls of the church. The words God gives His children to speak are reserved to be spoken before the rulers of society (St. Mark 13:11).

Figure this out. If we teach society the things of God, then God will be with us. The converse is also true. If we do not teach society the things of God, when we go to schools, governments, clubs, and even churches, God is not going to be with us. If we want God with us, the gospel must be preached in all places.

If you like the idea of beginning a *Christian Assertive Effort* in your church and community, duplicate the effort made by the early church in the book of Acts. God gave the author of the book of Acts, who was St. Luke, a perfect understanding of the Gospel Model from the very beginning (St. Luke 1:1).

The first Christians went to the synagogues, into the streets, to houses of noblemen, and public places with great success. They had the understanding that God and Christ must be viewed differently than other icons of faith. Jesus Christ was a living God. This required the Gospel Model, which is Christ. God through Christ was viewed uniquely and differently when first presented to society.

Understanding the Gospel Model can be equated with Martin Luther discovering that *the just must live by faith* (Romans 1:17). This fact was in the Bible for over fifteen hundred years but its undiscovered true meaning meant all the difference in the world. Martin Luther had his epiphany and every Protestant today has benefited by Luther's discovery.

Christians are expected to grow from one revelation of Christ to the next. Much is said about the "appearing of Christ" in the New Testament. More often than not, the appearing of Christ refers to what Christ said about being lifted up and thereby drawing men to Him rather than His eventual second coming. The whole and complete gospel is about the revelation of Jesus Christ. Christians are still learning of Christ, discovering a wonderful truth which Christ spent His ministry explaining. It is asked by Jesus for Christians to contribute to the appearing of Christ and to keep teaching about Him (2 Peter 3:18; Romans 16:25; 1 Corinthians 14:6; 2 Corinthians 12:1; Galatians 1:12; Galatians 2:2; Ephesians 1:17; Ephesians 3:3; Revelation 1:1).

Early Christians took a new awareness to the world, which is what Martin Luther did. Audiences that receive the initial instruction of the Gospel Model often become excited. "What do we do now?" they ask. Martin Luther learned all he could about *faith,* then he published his discovery for the world. To paraphrase the Great Commission, Jesus Christ said, "Learn of Me, keep receiving knowledge and epiphanies, and go into all of society teaching men of Me."

Christ wants us to use Him as a complete paradigm or model of psychological behavior, moral ethics, educational planning, and child rearing. Christ made it clear that He was the one and only way. Yet, scholars today have neglected to use Jesus as a behavioral model in schools, government, and society in general.

Revisit the true meaning of the Great Commission and you will find its true meaning has been skewed. The Great Commission was for Christians to target society for the publishing of the Word. This is the place to begin. Your first effort to sow the Word must begin here.

Maintenance is the term that has replaced the verb *to go* in the Great Commission. Keeping the Sunday school enrollment up, adding to the membership of the church, raising money to support and maintain the many programs, all these are good acts of maintenance but these are skewed one step away from fulfilling the Great Commission. Society has done more to affect the message of the church than the church has affected the humanistic message of society. Based on this, do you think there are better ways your church can carry out the Great Commission? Has the way of educating children changed in your community? Have school and government boards asked you to give them direction in developing ethics that match community values?

The *Christian Assertive Effort* does not seek to eliminate any plan you have for your church. The *Christian Assertive Effort* is simply Christians learning how to use Christ more efficiently. You do not need to reorganize the church. Most any form of organization will do or any program is good enough. The most important thing is to focus on the chief goal. At each public meeting, evaluate how the gospel has been taken into the community. You may find that your church is very much like Rev. Doe's church before he learned about the Gospel Model. If you see this, you are having an epiphany similar to Martin Luther's.

How to begin? Set aside a few evenings during the month to discuss the Gospel Model with your pastor or with a teacher that is dedicated to this new awakening. When it comes to learning something new, God's people get excited. In establishing a *Christian Assertive Effort* in your church or community, you can know from the beginning that no parent, teacher, principal, social worker, counselor, minister, any highly learned or unlearned person has ever failed while properly using the Gospel Model. The key word in this promise is *properly*. The scriptural task of the *Christian Assertive Effort* is to *train up children in the way they should go* (Proverbs 22:6).

CHAPTER TWO

The Gospel Model Is Real Religion

Proverbs 22:6: *Train up a child in the way he should go: and when he is old, he will not depart from it.*

Religion can work for parents, but it must be real religion. It must be something that people can trust and use. The power to raise children God's way is found by the utilization of the Gospel Model. The Gospel Model best explains the plan of God to assert Christ-like values into the heart of children and society. The theory is, if the Gospel Model is placed into the hearts of children, it will eventually arrive in society; and as children become adults, they will bring with them their Christian values. These children will use the Gospel Model to change the world.

The first chapters of this book are meant to quicken within parents and caretakers of children the expectations that something wonderful is about to happen to them and their children. As you learn about God's *way* of raising children with the Gospel Model, your life with children is going to improve. Simultaneously, you will feel empowered with confidence in how to deal with children when circumstances place them at risk.

The theme of this book is *raising children in the Bible way*. The way of raising children is spelled out to parents throughout the Bible and is found by using the Gospel Model like a pair of glasses. Through this view you observe and learn to train children. God promises in the Bible that parents will have success at raising children using the Gospel Model.

The way to raise children successfully is clearly spelled out to parents. Truth in raising children is plentiful, but Satan attempts to camouflage it. God expects his children, who want to raise children by the Bible, to search the Scriptures with the use of the Gospel Model.

> *Search the scriptures; for in them ye think ye have eternal life: and they are they which testify of me* (St. John 5:39).

> *Study to shew thyself approved unto God, a workman that needeth not to be ashamed, rightly dividing the word of truth* (2 Timothy 2:15).

The model for raising children is the good news Jesus Christ brought to the world. Christ is the model of everything good. Looking through Jesus makes everything clean and pure. Satan knows there is power in the Word of God and knows the children of God will be victorious as they follow God's examples of behavior in the Bible. God explains His *way* to His people. The Bible gives examples of parents accepting or rejecting God's *way* of raising children. There are examples of both a successful path and warnings of dangerous paths that children take.

As you search the Scriptures you will find two ways of raising children. One way is the Gospel Model. The other way is the one that only seems right. Proverbs 16:25 specifically states it: *There is a way that seemeth right unto a man, but the end thereof are the ways of death.* This is God's condemnation of humanism and naturalism, where man replaces God and becomes the authority for human morality.

The two ways are not easily distinguished since the Gospel Model has not been well defined in our churches and schools. Three basic characteristics make up the Gospel Model. These three characteristics define God's plan for parents in raising children. The first characteristic of the Gospel Model is seen when both parents and children know who they are by an active faith in God. It is not required that Christian parents have faith in man. But, faith in God separates this characteristic from humanism.

The second characteristic is that an active faith that changes society. Christians actually overcome the world. Since Christ came into the world, society has never been the same. The great men of God changed the world and we still talk about their religion today. What would our society be like without the preaching of Jesus Christ? While men of evil persuasion look for justifiable reasons to do evil, the example of Christ protects us and keeps us from violating the eternal laws of morality.

The third characteristic of the Gospel Model is that noble goals give purpose to living. Saint Paul said, *Set your affection on things above, not on things on the earth* (Colossians 3:2), which confirms what Jesus said in St. Matthew 6:20: *But lay up for yourselves treasures in heaven, where neither moth nor rust doth corrupt, and where thieves do not break through nor steal.* God wants man to aim high in setting goals.

Satan has an alternative model that mankind seems to believe is safe and intelligent to follow. It does seem right to many. Adherence to God's model is called GOALS—*God's Oriented Adaptable Life Style.* The other model is humanism and referred to as SINS—*Satan's Inadequate Naturalistic* (humanism) *Style.* The components of Satan's model are similar to the Gospel Model. Satan's model is humanism or naturalism and places man himself at the top of the authority structure, replacing God.

GOSPEL MODEL > GOALS > BEST CHANCE FOR SUCCESS
SEEMS RIGHT > SINS > DESTRUCTION_____

Parents, teachers, and churches, whose personal and professional behavior focuses on following the Gospel Model, find that raising children is less difficult and that looking towards the future is more pleasant. In the Old Testament when the children of Israel wandered in the desert, life was better for them when they followed the cloud by day and the pillar of fire by night. God provided a giant cloud by day and a burning fire at night as a model and a visible map. A cloud and a fire as a landmark showed the way with God's keeping power. His children could always look at these landmarks and keep from getting lost. It is a great virtue of parents to raise children who know where they are going.

Whenever the children of God did not follow the guide, they suffered greatly. Their children starved, they became thirsty, sickness entered the camp and they were defeated in battle. But as long as they followed God's *way*, God protected them from all these disasters. God made His children the envy of the world. All men knew Israel as the people of God. Visibly strong with a powerful God, they could defeat any god in the land. Religion really worked for Israel and the people of the world knew their religion was good.

Churches Lead *The Way*

The following letters illustrates the impact that can be made on parents when a church makes the effort to communicate the existence of God's plan for raising children.

(Letters From the Pastors)

Dear Parents,

It is the time of year that parents and children are excited about the beginning of another school term. Are you prepared for school? Run a checklist to see if your child has everything needed. Look for pencils, paper, books, clothing, and nametag with address and phone number, lunch box, a new hair cut, and a new pair of shoes. This stuff is important for children to look as if they belong and are ready to be accepted.

Make sure your checklist includes the protection and guidance of a heavenly angel. God has plenty of angels and wants to send one to school with every child. The guardian angel is a very loving spirit from God. There are also angels sent to school with children that are from the devil. God has provided a way for parents to raise children to know the good angels. We have worship services at our church designed to teach parents to send good angels to school with children. There is a special knowledge, which makes Proverbs 22:6 real. God's Word specializes in training parents to aid children. God prepares parents, then children.

To have good angels means to be protected by the shadow of the Almighty. Every good angel is mentally tough through a protecting armor of three basic concepts or "mindsets" from God's Word. These we hope to instill into the hearts of children. Children do not have to be consciously aware of these concepts to automatically respond to dangers brought on by the approaches of the devil.

Children who have basic Christian mindsets will have a higher incidence of being successful in school than other children. They have an armor against using drugs, bad language, fighting, stealing, and lies. Christian mindsets protect children from "at-risk factors" and make them better students, great citizens, and successful in life.

Our church assists parents in teaching these mindsets to children. Parents who have questions about how to raise children in today's world can come to church for this gospel. We want to share this wonderful knowledge with you.

Sincerely yours,
Pastor John Doe

Dear Parents,

Recently you have been informed that your teenage students would have to learn to be tolerant of lifestyles that offend your Christian values. The use of drugs and promiscuous sexual behavior are associated with these lifestyles. It is no surprise that violent behavior, stealing, attitudes of opposition and gang affiliations are trying to take over the place where teens are educated. Many parents have placed children in private schools in response to deteriorating conditions in the public schools and their movement towards humanistic beliefs.

Not every parent is in a position to send children to private schools. We offer a special support to parents and help children and teenagers to overcome the many factors that put them at risk. Our religious programming helps parents immunize teenagers from the many social diseases that exist. You can have control of your teens' behavior to guide them in making the correct choices. The Bible really does offer parents a way to deal with teens.

Please tell parents about the effort that we are making at our church to assist them in dealing with at-risk children. The Word of God does have answers for parents who need to reach out to their children and change their behaviors. We want to help.

Sincerely,
John Doe, Jr.

(Sample Letter from Church Leader)

Dear Church Member:

Changes that have taken place recently in society and more recently in our local public school seem to have shut out Christian values and replaced them with a humanistic philosophy. We are told that this philosophy is more in tune with our national values of separation of church and state. This, however, is a great misunderstanding. Your Christian values are the values that are in step with the Constitution of the United States and other national creeds and documents.

Our church will be offering a series of in-service meetings for public school teachers and parents who want to teach their Christian values without offending other religious beliefs. Christian beliefs can be correctly asserted back into the local school system and society by using the correct teaching model.

A planned and united effort of all Christians will restore our national values to public living. Our first lesson will be Monday night. Invite any Christian teacher who needs our help or any concerned parent who would like to assist in spreading the gospel into the schools.

Sincerely,
Fred Stone, Lay-leader

(Letters From Parents)

Dear Pastor John Doe,

Thank you for reaching out to my children and me. It was wonderful to discover that I could be in control of my children's thoughts and behavior. It sounds like a contradiction that my husband and I are in control of children who think for themselves. But, it is true. They did learn from us to make the right decisions. My fifth grader turned his life around almost overnight. His grades changed from F to A. He actually went to the top of his class and scored one of the highest scores on his school achievement test. He has been chosen for the Duke University Talent Search Team. Isn't that great! Last year I was asking the school to retain him in the fifth grade.

Our seventh grader has chosen a better peer group with which she now loafs. She did join the Junior Beta Club and has actually found delight in doing things for others. The attitude of opposition to parents is gone. She really has learned to enjoy her youth group at church.

Fred made the high school basketball team and will be the starting guard when the season begins. He also made first chair on the debate team. This does not seem like that old Fred who was so shy and reserved. Before we used the tips you gave us from the Word of God to motivate children to success, we thought Fred would be a follower. That really bothered us.

By the way, my husband and I have grown so much in the Lord. The spiritual assistance we gave our children has made us better Christians, happier, and motivated to do more for others. If you have a job that needs to be done in the church, please call on us. We want to work for the Lord now that we are a healed family.

Sincerely yours,
Connie Tabor

Dear Pastor,

Thank you for the wonderful learning tips your committee on *The Christian Assertive Effort* gave to my wife and me. The problems we thought we were seeing in Amy have disappeared just as you told us they would. Amy now sleeps the entire night and is eating well. Her energy level has really made her active. In a couple of years when she begins school, we think she will be ready.

Sincerely,
The Scotts

The above letters certainly indicate this church and pastor is involved with the community and its many families. The church knows what it is doing and is telling the community that it has the answers to problems parents have. Here, people view their church and pastor as an assertive force in their lives. An assertive spirit, making the church more appealing and trustworthy in evangelism, creates a positive public image of the church. Can you see the many appealing features of an assertive church that would make parents and grandparents want to attend? Hundreds of neglected parents would love to receive or be able to write a letter like the above. Do non-churchgoers have a special reason to attend your church?

While you are thinking of the wonderful features of Rev. John Doe's church, try to imagine what changes would need to take place in your pastor and congregation to make your church like Rev. Doe's church. It is very possible for teachers and pastors to receive letters of thanks from thankful parents. The caretakers of children in Rev. Doe's church followed a specific *way*—the Gospel Model— in expressing their concern about children. From my experience as both a pastor and elementary school principal, the Gospel Model for raising children always produced grateful responses.

What is the Gospel Model? It is Jesus Christ, who says He is the *way* (St. John 14:6). The Scriptures say many things about Christians walking in the way. The following is a medley of verses taken from the Book of Isaiah that illustrate that Jesus is the *way* and is to be followed as a pattern of righteousness to bring understanding and deliverance to the people of the world. Take time to read these about the way of God. Isaiah 30:21; 35:8; 40:3; 40:14; 48:17; 49:9; 57:14.

There is little doubt that God wants His people to follow the *way* that makes up the Gospel Model. God saw Himself as the model of righteousness and defined Himself as such. In the book of Exodus 3:14, God was asked whom He was who sent Moses to deliver God's people: *And God said unto Moses, I AM THAT I AM: and he said, Thus shalt thou say unto the children of Israel, I AM hath sent me unto you.*

In the Old Testament several names were given to God and each depended on what God was doing at the time. For example, God was the Deliverer when He protected the children of Israel from the Egyptians and later from the Moabites. He was the God of Peace in tranquil times in Israel. Whatever God was doing, He was.

The Gospel Model (Save-er) Died for Our Sins To Save Us I Am What I Do To This End—Goal

The Gospel Model requires the taking of Christ into society. There is no model without the action or doing. It is planting the seeds of righteousness in schools, PTA's, the country club, families, and in the hearts of parents and children. Pastor Doe's church was busy doing this—taking the Gospel Model to the lives of people. People who were touched by the model returned to the church to make the church more productive.

Parents would rather attend a church that makes the effort to empower parents to avoid a disastrous experience of child rearing.

Our Bible teaches us that we must do good when we know what good is. Parental resentment is fostered if parents find out too late that the church had a special knowledge to help parents but did not share it. A sad experience is to see the disappointment on the faces of parents who have just realized that they could have saved their children from failure, if they had only known what to do. This is unacceptable to the assertive church.

Can you recall hearing a single sermon on the subject of raising children by the Gospel Model? Instruction in the Gospel Model is not there. The church needs to begin its training mission with parents and train them in godly parenting skills that are found in the Bible (Titus 2:3b, *teachers of good things*). A church, which believes that its evangelism must begin with the youth, does not exactly follow God's plan for growth. God always begins the building up of powerful youth by first training great parents. Great children soon follow.

The Christian ministry has neglected the area of parental training and, thereby, has lost a great harvest. Opportunity is here. A neglected population now seeks help in child rearing. The church should be the place where these seekers find help, making the Christian community a place for a new awakening, a quickening, and a new attendance.

Schools and the Gospel Model

When we presented the concept of raising children the Bible way in the public schools, the successes created caused parents and teachers from other school districts to seek out these methods for their schools and children. Among the needy—parents who had children classified as being at risk—the word spread like wildfire as they sought out the source of this seemingly new effort. As might be expected, those who did not believe their children were at risk did not see the need to be involved in the effort to work a program for at-risk children. Many who ignored this effort missed the chance to strengthen and immunize their children against future failures.

The 100 percent effectiveness of the Bible methods of training parents and children caught the attention of Charter Ridge Hospital (a system of hospitals that has schools and residences for children and adolescents who have emotional disorders). The school principal was invited to share his ideas at the annual Children in Crisis Conference. One local parent, who used the Gospel Model with her son while she waited for Charter Ridge to provide residential space for him, found that when he was to be admitted, the psychiatrist judged her son no longer needed to be admitted. The mother was instructed to return home and to continue using the methods she had been using. Since that time several teachers and parents have used the Gospel Model of behavior with children who suffered from serious emotional problems. God's truth was powerful in this area.

The local newspaper did several articles on the success our school was having in dealing with children who had special problems. The publicity caught the attention of parents and caretakers of children from surrounding areas. We gave them information on how to use models without telling them that the information of other models was channeled through the greatest model—the Gospel Model.

The point is that when the Word of God is introduced to society, regardless how it is worded, the world will improve. Society remains hungry for the gospel. Success in using the Bible methods of caring for children brings a neglected population to the church for a positive needs fulfillment. God still does miracles, and miracles do bring people to the source of miracles.

As throngs of people were drawn to Christ, He continued to heal them. The spirit of Christ is a quickening spirit. That is what Pastor John Doe discovered and that is the reason people wanted to attend his church and why parents wanted their children in Principal Pal's school.

The healing of youth of social diseases has been a low priority to many churches, although throngs of people still scramble for physical healing by faith healers. To participate in a deeper, more spiritual healing is to get into the hearts of children and change their lives. This is the true meaning of the words of Jesus when He commanded His disciples to allow little children to come to Him (St. Luke 18:16).

Heal one dysfunctional family or save one at-risk child and your church will gain the type of fame that drew crowds to Jesus. They came to our elementary school for special help because there was not a school in their community that was offering the Word of God as redemption and salvation in parenting. Jesus told His disciples that they would do greater miracles than He did. There is no greater miracle than to heal a sick child. An assertive effort with the Gospel Model will attract the attention of those who have real needs.

As Pastor John Doe wrote to the parents in his church, God is able to send angels to school with children. Angels do appear throughout life to make announcements. The Bible teaches people are not aware of these angels (Hebrews 13:2). Parents need to know how the angels of light work. Does your church make clear the family plan sent to us by God? If not, it is time to make the effort to help your church do so.

CHAPTER THREE

Results Now!
Quick Success

Proverbs 22:6: *Train up a child . . . he will not depart from it.*

The understanding of the Gospel Model was an unbelievable journey of quick successes with children and parents. Our quick successes occurred with families whose children were at risk emotionally, socially, and educationally. These happened almost instantly. After a single candle was lit within me, it was so easy to light the candles of parents who were seeking the light.

Academically, there are several models used to address the needs of children. The knowledge of valid behavioral models can be channeled through the Gospel Model. Jesus said in St. John 14:6: *I am the way, the truth, and the life: no man cometh unto the Father, but by me.* The research of famous psychologists is a validation of what the Bible teaches about child rearing. It is likely that you will recognize the components and terminology from these different models as we mention different researchers of the truth. They have parts of God's model in that they have discovered truth.

Dr. Martin Seligman is the author of the learned helplessness theory, theories on depression, human development, adaptive and maladaptive explanatory lifestyles, and of several books. He has made a tremendous contribution to teaching people how to be successful in life. Two most recent books, *Helplessness* and *Learned Optimism* have been best sellers. Dr. Seligman's theories have been published in college textbooks and used in clinical settings to treat depression and other forms of mental illnesses. We recommend these books as important supplemental reading in using the Gospel Model.

The power of the Gospel Model by way of the learned helplessness theory is to convert *learned helplessness* in children to an enabling life force of adaptive behavior. Learning adaptive behavior has an immunizing effect on children against failure, depression, and giving up. The power of the truth that comes from scientific research comes from the fact that all truth originates from God. Research and good science simply discover the same truth.

Science has discovered in the depressed lives of children the same thing the Word of God referred to as *evil coming from a heart* (St. Matthew 12:35). The best theories of human behavior are simply facts about behavior that the Bible has always exposed. If the Bible is anything, it is a discussion of models of maladaptive behavior and adaptive behavior.

Professional educators and psychologist use a number of models to do their work. Teachers are familiar with Bloom's Taxonomy. Two key terms in this model are *cognitive domain* and *affective domain*, which have special meanings for teachers. Many teachers use the Bloom's Taxonomy to target teaching.

The terms *id, ego,* and *super ego* are important components of the psychoanalytic model of Sigmoid Freud, whereas *learned helplessness* is a model used by Martin Seligman to study depressed children. The Gospel Model is the best model to channel all models through to be used to raise children in the Bible way.

At the elementary school, parents were able to train their children to become successful by using models. Parents came to identify two different lifestyles that allowed them to intervene emotionally, educationally, and morally with their children that were either mildly, moderately, or severely at risk. These parents had 100 percent success rates in controlling the emotional development of their children.

Parents kept coming to school for help. Nothing had worked and it was time to try something new. We gave the effort which boiled down to parents having the Gospel Model explained by using Martin Seligman's adaptive and maladaptive explanatory lifestyle to substitute for what Christ called a pure heart and a corrupt heart (St. Luke 6:25). Children either lived like they were going to be successful or not successful. We taught them to live the style of life that led to success.

Parents listened to something new since all else had failed. A new approach demands the attention of a real unsolved problem. It was so easy. We adhered to just basic terminology and made references to what research had indicated. We demonstrated how the Gospel Model could be brought out of the laboratory and into the lives of children. The parents simply planned a strategy as to how they would alter their children's explanatory lifestyle from maladaptive to adaptive. To put this in religious terms, we transformed their lives by renewing their minds.

An explanatory lifestyle is the way people explain life events. You identify an explanatory lifestyle when you identify a person as being an optimist or pessimist, generous or stingy, brave or cowardly, and benevolent or hateful. People are familiar with lifestyles. These represent ways of thinking.

And be not conformed to this world: but be ye transformed by the renewing of your mind, that ye may prove what is that good, and acceptable, and perfect, will of God. (Romans 12:2)

Quick Success I: William, the "spoiled brat syndrome"

From Martin Seligman's book *Helplessness* we compared the behavioral symptoms of sixth grade student William with the characteristics Seligman described as the "spoiled brat syndrome." A decision was made to intervene to extinguish the symptoms of a depressed personality, which controlled the behavior of William.

William had entered our elementary school as a third grade student, having moved from Louisville, Kentucky, where he had been academically screened and was considered a candidate for the academically gifted program. As a first grader, William was intellectually strong. Learning came easy. He sat in class and effortlessly soaked up everything. The second grade was almost a repeat of the first grade, except there was no longer a large academic gap between William and other top students in the class, a distinction the parents of William recognized but were not overly concerned with.

William began the third grade of school in Louisville and finished the last twelve weeks of the school year at our school. Williams mother voiced her concerns to the third grade teacher that William had made little progress and was actually falling behind the rest of the class. The lack of achievement was attributed to disturbances associated with a child moving to a new community. William was promoted to the fourth grade with the expectation that his gifted intellectual ability would come through and he would adjust.

The fourth grade year was a bitter disappointment to William's mother. Her son became dysphoric, lacked motivation, wandered aimlessly about the school during recess as if he were lost, was not interested in cultivating friendships, or in completing academic tasks. The spirit of competition left William; he became noticeably passive and had few relationships with students his own age. Achievement test results revealed that William was working at a low average level but not low enough to qualify for remedial classes. William was certainly not living up to his parents' original expectations of a gifted child. The school had no solutions or answers for these parents.

Frustrations continued to add up during the fifth grade year. William was referred for testing for special classes. Maybe he qualified for a Learning Disability Unit? He did not. Another abysmal year passed. William's mother wanted to do something, anything, to rescue her child. She approached the principal at the beginning of the sixth grade year with a desperate statement: "We have decided that William is too immature to go to the sixth grade this year. He's just not ready to go on. It's not the school's fault or any fault of the teachers. It's just that William needs more time to mature. Can we keep him in the fifth grade another year?"

What the principal had learned from his work with the Gospel Model had changed how the principal viewed the educational progress of William, whose behavior was telling the principal that something could be done to change William's style of responding to school. There was a plan. It was time to intervene. There was a sense of urgency and assurance in the response of the principal that a solution existed.

It is important that parents sense and believe you know what works. Remember this, if a child is emotionally at risk, the factors that created the situation will likely be present in the person closest to the at-risk child. The parents had contributed greatly to the failing process of William.

"No!" The principal said this with firm conviction. "William does not need to be held back. His problem is not immaturity. William should be making good grades. I think I know what his problem is. Things will be better this year."

That was the first time the principal had seen William's mother smile. She believed and expected to hear a better and newer plan. This was new hope for her. A positive side effect of helping children overcome emotional risk factors is that generally the whole family is helped. It is difficult to emotionally assist a child without rendering assistance to those about him.

To reinforce the seed of hope it was important to present solid and believable evidence of a reason for hope. The following explanation by the principal did the job. "William behaves as if he has learned helplessness, which is a form of a learned depressed personality. The tendency to become depressed is an inherited characteristic, either physically or socially. Children with a predisposition to be depressed are more susceptible to be discouraged due to even minor stressful life events. They lose self-confidence easily and develop a helpless self-image. In William's case he appears to have all the classic symptoms of what has been called the 'spoiled brat syndrome' by Dr. Seligman. This learning can be extinguished and replaced with a newly learned adaptable explanatory lifestyle." The explanation to William's mother about explanatory styles and learned helplessness took about thirty minutes.

In most cases one or both of the parents of children who are developing within the frame of a depressed personality syndrome knows the stress factor(s) that initiated the development of the depressed personality. They also know the general time that the child began to be influenced or taken over by depressed personality. Since such factors tend to have occurred under unpleasant circumstances, it is a natural cognitive response to have forgotten depressive factors. By pointing out several general factors, precursors, that are known to depress the behavior of children, the parent may recall forgotten information. When such information is recalled, the parent will intuitively grasp a better understanding of the problem and often become very receptive to advice. The giver of advice does not have to know all the personal stress factors in a family to be able to follow the Gospel Model in giving advice.

"Your son appears as if he might develop a depressed personality as he becomes an adult. At this time, he appears to have learned how not to learn. Your son is more like you believed him to be when he was in the first grade. With a few simple methods used at home, he should shortly return to a high level of learning." This statement of assurance, with which William's mother could make a positive identification, and with a proposed plan of action leading to positive results, almost immediately led to the removal of a depressed atmosphere of leaning at William's home.

William did not need medical treatment for depression. His mother did, however, consult with a doctor, a trained therapist, who confirmed that William's problem had been identified. William needed to learn how to learn by attacking academic problems and staying with the problems until the learning tasks were completed. In first grade, the high intelligence of William made learning easy, in fact, effortless. As the learning difficulty increased through the grades, William did not put forth the effort needed to achieve higher intellectual levels. Somewhere the parents of William had neglected to keep bringing up the child in the way he needed to go. Proverbs 22:6 does not allow a resting-place for parents. Their motto should have been, "Keep training this bright child." You cannot afford to relax in training children.

Essentially, this is what Martin Seligman was saying in his discussion of the spoiled brat syndrome, that a person could learn helplessness and a passive responsive nature. Martin Seligman has presented a very strong argument for "helplessness" as a model for depression, which allowed these parents to have a better view of how their child was developing.

However, at school and in church, we are not dealing with depression as a clinical topic. Seligman often does. We use Seligman's model as a learning model to spot the need to teach children an adaptable explanatory lifestyle. The Gospel Model is a learning model and is at the top of the learning curve. The Gospel Model takes other models beyond the scientists' understanding and makes these more usable by less trained persons.

William's family did things at home to build a positive explanatory lifestyle. William worked with a computer to learn to complete problem solving tasks. At school he had a plan to bring his grades from "D" and "F" to the "A" level. In casual conversation with this boy in the hall of the school, the principal told him how capable he really was and that he should be making all "A" grades. William had a growth in confidence and informed the principal that in a few days his grades would improve. "In a little time," he said, "I'll be making all 'A' grades." With these words William demonstrated his growing confidence. This was his active faith taking hold of his life. William's home was a Christian home that now used the Gospel Model.

Progress was on the way! At the end of his sixth grade year, William won the school math award. The next year William was selected to the Duke University Talent Search Team. On his sixth grade achievement test, William scored in the ninety-nine percentiles in reading and math. This indicated that he had recovered from the three years of intellectual failure. Was this not simple? His parents only needed the Gospel Model as a way to view William's emotional development; then a lot of common sense methods worked.

Quick Success II: Learned Depressed Personality

Matthew was simply not motivated to do fourth grade schoolwork or socialize with other children. He was a member of the Cub Scouts but did not seem to enjoy the activities of scouting.

The Cub Scout leader had to force Matthew to mix with the den. After six weeks of school Matthew's parents had reason to be concerned about their child's low grades. They came to school to discuss the learning problems Matthew was having. They wanted the school to do something to help Matthew, although they had no idea what this something would be.

They were looking for the reasons that Matthew was not learning. The teacher felt Matthew needed more help at home. Matthew's mother could not accept this explanation since most of her time was spent encouraging her son and going over his schoolwork. During the parent-teacher conference, the teacher kept throwing out suggestions as to why Matthew was not doing well in school, and the parents kept countering each suggestion with an explanation of why the suggestion would not work.

"We have a set time for Matthew to do his homework. We make sure Matthew is in bed by 9:00 P.M. He gets a sugar-free breakfast each morning. We purchase educational games for him to work with on his computer. When he brings home bad grades, he is grounded."

The teacher promised to call home more quickly with the first sign of academic trouble with Matthew. The parents promised to provide more study time for Matthew at home. The teacher returned to her classroom; from the expression on the faces of the parents, it was obvious to the principal that nothing had been resolved that would lead to Matthew's improvement.

The principal knew students who were not motivated to learn were often discovered to be depressed. Even if children are not depressed, traits of depression are more contagious than a common cold. Children learn to copy the behavior of depressed persons with whom they have come in frequent contact. This means that the causal relationship of children not learning in school could be found in the home.

The learned depressed personality syndrome is more common than the common cold. It is more contagious than the common cold. Learned depression is generally a quiet behavior and can be easily unnoticed. In a school crowd of several hundred children, this is not so true, as these children tend to be grouped together into small crowds, isolated, where they can readily be identified. They are often identified as discipline problems and slow learners.

When not sure of what behavior is appropriate, children often behave as if they are depressed. They may not know what behavior is needed to secure reinforcement for future successful learning. If the reinforcement does not come, future learning is retarded. In other words, children need a clear signal from their parents that their behavior is good. Matthew was not getting this attention and it had made him sad.

"Mr. Hankins," the principal said, "your son acts as if he has leaned the behavior of a depressed person. What do you know about depression in children? Are you aware that children can learn to behave in a depressed manner?"

Mr. Hankins answered, "Oh! That never occurred to me, but since you mentioned it, that may be the thing."

This was an important time in the lives of the Hankins family. Recognition of a problem that existed in Matthew's life was recognition of a problem that was true of the complete family. Matthew learned his behavior from his family and he exhibited depressed behavior. He was not clinically depressed; he had simply learned a low response attitude.

When we use the word depressed, a nauseous stigma is attached. It might be better to simply to say one is sad. Sometimes I am depressed from watching a sad program on television. It is possible for persons to stay sad for a long period of time; this type of sadness is not healthy. It is possible to be sad over a period of time and not be aware of the cause of the sadness. For example, not being in control of a situation can make one sad, which was the case of the Hankins parents. Not being in control was teaching this child bad feelings and keeping him from learning better and suitable behaviors.

"What can we do?" Mr. Hankins asked.

The principal had picked up on the fact that this husband and wife did not agree on how children were to be raised. The father favored a strict disciplined approach, and the mother was prone to pet and give in to the childish demands of Matthew. Matthew was not in control of his feelings and did not understand clearly how he was to behave. This was also true of his parents.

Sound advice was forth coming. "You need to come to an understanding of how you want to raise Matthew. You two disagree on things. He is confused and unable to concentrate on his work. He does not smile and laugh very often, and he does not make friends easily. New information on child rearing may help you to agree with each other on an approach different from what each of you now take. I recommend you read a book called *Parent Power* by John Rosemond that really has some good ideas. This book has helped several of our parents. I suggest you purchase this book and read it. It will offer new ideas which you may find useful."

The principal explained that the idea was to give Matthew a way of being in control, which could be brought about by using strategies that both parents agreed upon, which would prompt responses guided by one point of view. Matthew's world could then be understood by him and changed to please what his parents wanted. Simply stated, the theory was that Matthew needed to be trained in one way of responding. By this the child could learn to control the important areas of his life, the areas deemed important by his parents, who he naturally wanted to please. Matthew's parents began to build an adaptive explanatory style (the Gospel Model) for both themselves and their child. This adaptable style was explained to the Hankins family. Mr. and Mrs. Hankins left the principal's office after promising to read *Parent Power* and the material the principal provided about maladaptive and adaptive explanatory lifestyles and examples of how these styles worked. *Parent Power* provides several suggested strategies that can be used to place parents in control of the family, thereby establishing a way for the child to direct his behavior and gain control of himself.

The school did not hear from the Hankins family until four months had passed. In the meantime, Matthew's teacher said to the principal, "Whatever Matthew's parents did, they started a fire under him. His grades are much improved and he is really working."

The Cub Scout leader responded also. "The biggest change has occurred in Matthew. He is actually enjoying himself. Where did all this laughter and fun come from all of a sudden?"

The point to this observation is that changes can be made in children's behavior and others will notice this change but not know how or why the change took place. The Hankins family had done something different that quickly changed the quality of the life of their son.

There were things in the Hankins family that were not initially shared with the school. One big event, which told Matthew that his parents were not in control, was his behavior at bedtime. He had captured the attention of his mother by not allowing her to leave his bedside until he fell asleep. However long it took him to go to sleep, the mother had to stay by his side. If she left for any reason, Matthew cried and cried. The mother felt guilty as if she had abandoned him and soon returned to his bedside. This had gone on for a number of years with Matthew. After reading of a similar situation in *Parent Power*, the mother attempted the same strategy outlined by John Rosemond with remarkable results. One well-planned session with her son and Mrs. Hankins was free. She broke through to Matthew, and her son sensed his mother was taking control of the family.

The success of this mother in this one area had wonderful side effects; successes began to multiply. Mr. and Mrs. Hankins' relationship with each other improved. They began to agree on what should be done for Matthew and how he should behave. Matthew began to show the results of a new explanatory style; his improved behavior at home was helping him to be successful at school.

The principal learned several interesting facts by observing the improvement in the Hankins family. (1) Helping the Hankins family was simply a matter of letting them know where to find correct information. Sometimes it only takes a small push in the right direction to turn a depressing situation completely around. (2) The idea that others had similar problems and had received help from reading new information gave Mr. and Mrs. Hankins encouragement to attempt the same with the same favorable results. (3) And, parental influence is greater than the influence of other authority figures such as Cub Scout leaders and teacher. Clearly parents were the primary influence on Matthew's school behavior as well as his social behavior. The teacher may have thought her initial advice was the reason for the change. The Scout leader may have believed his efforts to force Matthew to mix with other Cub Scouts was the reason. Clearly the parents deserve all the credit.

One last observation that must not be overlooked is that the Hankins family was free to use a variety of information and resources, many of which can be useful in helping parents find a way to teaching an adaptable and biblical explanatory style in children. *The point is that if parents are aware of this style, it guides them in choosing materials and methods that will lead to creating in children the style and mindset of responding with automatic successful behavior.* Notice that the success pattern in Matthew's life began with his mother regaining control, which continued in his school and scouting life. The principal did not have to be told a large number of embarrassing family situations to be helpfully involved.

Quick Success III: A Misplaced Child

Children who are reacting emotionally to crisis situations sometimes exhibit bizarre behavior, which repulses teachers and other persons who are the ones in a position to help. If the teacher is emotionally unstable or not properly prepared to deal with bizarre emotional behavior, the end result can be that the teacher fails to have compassion toward the emotionally stressed child.

Schools always have a few teachers on staff who can only teach children who are well adjusted, come from the correct social class, or are intelligent. For this reason, emotionally at-risk students often become trapped in the placement shuffle and end up in a program that offers the least resistance.

In Kentucky the easiest class for the emotionally at-risk children to fall into was the Transition Class. The purpose of the class was to provide students who had fallen behind in math and reading the opportunity to catch up with the normal class without having to be retained in the first and second grade. Very few protective guidelines existed to keep children from being put away in these classes. If a student was identified by a previous achievement test as needing remedial instruction in math or reading, these classes were offered to these children. Parents could refuse to allow children to be placed in the Transition Class. Admission and Release Committees were not involved, as the class was not intended to serve special education students or emotionally disturbed children. Informed parents did not allow their children in these classes. However, emotionally at-risk and marginally intelligent children ran a higher risk of not having parents who were in the know about school placement. It is the emotionally at-risk children who ended up in the Transition Class. Principals and teachers are duty bound to disallow such a placement.

If a principal supervised a teacher who did not want to deal with an emotionally at-risk child, the Transition Class offered the principal a tempting solution. As a principal, I quickly learned that most often the only persons who cared about intervening to stop children from failure were parents. Teachers would not do it. Guidance counselors would not do it. Principals would not do it. School superintendents would not do it. Chances are that if parents are unable to arm themselves with the knowledge of when and how to intervene, intervention will not occur and their children run the risk of being locked up in such classes.

Ryan Ferguson had been a first grade student in the city schools. His mother and father had separated just before school started in August. Ryan and his first grade teacher clashed violently. The teacher viewed Ryan as immature, insecure, and a discipline problem. The teacher spanked Ryan twelve times before Christmas, always as a last resort (this is sarcasm on my part in case you missed it). After each spanking Ryan failed to show improved behavior. In fact, things deteriorated (wonder why?) to a crisis situation. The teacher admitted to Mrs. Ferguson and the school principal that she could do nothing for Ryan because of his undisciplined behavior.

The principal witnessed the twelve spankings, which were accompanied by long lectures on manners and respect for authority. Several times the principal scolded Ryan as an alternative to spanking. Most of Ryan's recesses and play times were withheld.

Ryan had no friends and hated school. All agreed something had to be done.

After Christmas vacation Ryan was placed in the Transition Class with other students who were not learning. Upset, hidden away with the school's failures, Ryan waited the year out. Ryan's mother and father patched up their marriage and Ryan was promoted to the second grade Transition Class. What a joke!

Two weeks after the beginning of the next school year Ryan's family moved into the County School District. Ryan attempted to enroll in the school where he belonged. However, there was not a Transition Class at this school. The guidance counselor, acting on a letter from the city school principal that stated Ryan needed to be in a Transition Class, sent Ryan to our school without reviewing test results, evaluation criteria, or school records. The message came through very clearly to the county schools that Ryan was a discipline problem and did not fit in well with the normal classes. The elementary school principal was absent when Ryan was placed in his school. Mr. Pal had been attending a conference called *Children in Crisis* sponsored by Charter Ridge Hospitals who were noted for dealing with emotional disorders of children and adolescents.

Upon his return the principal found this child all over the walls and in the floor of the classroom. Ryan was totally out of control and appeared to have no idea of how he was to behave in school. The principal phoned Ryan's old school, talked to the first grade teacher and the principal. It was obvious, Ryan had been placed in the Transition Class as an attempt to manage his behavior. Ryan clearly mirrored the depressed personality syndrome and had fallen into the placement shuffle. For the last two years the people who managed Ryan's emotional growth had done nothing to help him. Do you think Ryan had reason to be depressed?

Mrs. Ferguson was very apprehensive about being called to come to school for a parent conference after only one day of her son's attendance. "Mrs. Ferguson," said the principal, "Ryan doesn't belong in the Transition Class but he is in need of having a complete first grade year in a supportive atmosphere without the distraction of depressed attitudes to influence his emotional development."

The principal continued: "I have found out by calling the city school that Ryan was placed in the Transition Class for discipline, not for a learning scheme."

Mrs. Ferguson was very upset at first and did not listen too well. "Just where does Ryan belong, Mr. Pal?" It was a sharp, bitter question.

The reply came: "The people who have been in charge of Ryan had no plans to help Ryan so he ended up at the place of least resistance. No plan existed for Ryan's education other than getting him out of the way. Mrs. Ferguson, do you have a plan or know of one that includes your son progressing beyond the first grade?"

The answer was a somber, "No."

The principal continued: "Believe me! I know what I am talking about. This is going to be the most important day of your lives. You will have the truth. Ryan does not need to be bused across the county to school. He's a smart child who has not been given a chance to learn. Instead he has learned to be depressed. Let's put him in the first grade at a school close to home. I'll call the principal and ask for a special placement in the first grade for your son. Let's make some plans for Ryan. Let's plan to make him see things differently. School should not be like Ryan has experienced it."

Ryan's mother was given a clear explanation of the adaptive explanatory style. This took about fifteen minutes of the principal's time. The adaptable explanatory style was explained and outlined.

It was important for Ryan to correctly explain things in a positive manner, in a manner that gave Ryan control of how to explain the world so he could use school experiences to shape his future, rather than allowing school experiences to depress him.

Briefly, the Gospel Model for raising children was explained to Mrs. Ferguson. Everything she heard was something positive about what could be done for Ryan. It was believable and changed the learning atmosphere at Ryan's home. Four months later Mrs. Ferguson called the elementary school to thank Mr. Pal. Her son was a model student. It was too good to be true. Ryan was learning, playing, and loving. What a wonderful day all had the day Mrs. Ferguson called.

William, Matthew, and Ryan are well-adjusted adults today. Had we not intervened first with the parents by imparting information to them, there is no doubt that William, Matthew, and Ryan would have been less successful in life. Although they might have tried, it is not likely other teachers or principals would have intervened with the necessary information. Of course, there are many teachers and principals who do great things in the lives of children, but there is something special about a situation that looks otherwise hopeless when the Word of God intervenes. Think of the number of parents that you may have been able to help, if you had only been familiar with the Gospel Model. The amount of time spent with these parents was, on the average, less than thirty minutes. It did not take a giant effort, just a little effort.

CHAPTER FOUR

"In the Beginning"— The History

Proverbs 22:6: *Train up a child in the way he should go: and when he is old, he will not depart from it.*

My mother taught me the Gospel Model as a small child. She did not use the vocabulary being used here, but she provided the content for the necessary thinking that helped me overcome poor self-esteem and a depressed personality. I did not know what college was at age four, but I sure wanted to go there. Mother put this and other noble goals in my head early. Even during the discouraging times when I was a very poor student, I never gave up the goal of graduating from college.

This was remarkable since I did not learn to read until my second year of high school. I was retained in the third and fifth grade and could not recite the alphabet until the second year in the third grade. I was only five when I entered the first grade as a depressed child and became more so as I was passed through to the second and third grades. You would have never predicted my end from what I was as a child. The Gospel Model saved me.

Discovering the Gospel Model was truly a compilation of a lifetime of experiences beginning at a very early age. Without the

Gospel Model being instilled in my heart, the knowledge that I am able to share with others would not be possible. My father, who was greatly missed, had been killed in 1944 in France, during World War II.

Information leading to the complete discovery of the Gospel Model began in the year of 1958. At the age of 16, I was a very unhappy adolescent. From the time of my father's death, my mother had been depressed. I had learned from this situation what the professionals now call a *depressed personality syndrome*; therefore I responded to life events in a very negative manner. In tears I asked a mature Christian brother, Charles Fields, "Why do I feel so unhappy and sad? Why does God allow me to suffer such pain?"

How to escape from my horrific loneliness and sadness was my problem. The feelings of rejection were unbelievable. My suffering was from a depressed personality syndrome. We know now that about seven percent of all school children feel this way.

Charles Fields answered, "Son, I do not know why you feel or why you suffer so, but I am sure God has a reason for all this. It may be that when you are grown, some small child will ask this question to you and because you have suffered this pain, you may know the correct answer to stop the pain in others."

Praise God, the prophetic words of Charles Fields came true many times and hopefully will be true for a long time to come. Some people are depressed their entire lives without knowing what it is that makes them unhappy while a few others find salvation and deliverance from the darkness.

There are levels and degrees of unhappiness for children. Some suffer mildly, others moderately, and a few suffer severely. The objective of teaching the Gospel Model is to enlighten parents to the fact that children do not need to suffer mental anguish at all.

Hopefully an understanding of the Gospel Mode will enable you to sense the mental suffering some children are now going through.

All of our Quick Success children experienced confusion, sadness, rejection, low self-esteem, lack of motivation, and the prompting to give up. The reason the case studies of William, Matthew, and Ryan were presented in the previous chapter was to demonstrate how powerful the Gospel Model is.

There is such a thing as therapeutic suffering. The correct type of suffering makes children and adults stronger. Depressed suffering destroys the soul. When children are growing and learning in *the way* of God, they learn to overcome problems. Problems become stepping stones, which becomes a way to step out of the darkness. Children need to be shown where the stepping stones are so they can walk on water. The Gospel Model or the *way* will point this out to children when instilled in their hearts.

Many great men have suffered from depression all their lives, but in spite of it have been successful, helpful, and gentle like Abraham Lincoln. Others, like Adolph Hitler, have been monsters. Children can become many things while enduring unhappiness. Childhood should and can be a time when evil days do not come. But, the evil days will come for many regardless of what parents do. However, parents do not have to fail by not teaching children a *way* to overcome emotional stresses. That is what my mother did for me. She wanted to shelter me from suffering but could not. She was left with the option of teaching me that I was not allowed to give up, and that I had to set noble goals.

Without knowledge of *the way*, things will only get worse. With the Gospel Model instilled in a child, there is great hope. To me Abraham Lincoln is a great example of a low mood child being taught *the way* of God by a wonderful stepmother. When he was of age, he used his suffering to set men free just like Moses did.

Somehow God guided me through college and into a teaching career, an elementary school principal's position, and now into the ministry of the United Methodist Church. My mother deserves much credit for my success. Although both of us were depressed, she structured my mind to learn in a manner or style that allowed me to overcome my depression.

As a teacher and principal, this knowledge that children were unhappy and unsuccessful haunted me. Year after year children would begin school. Each year it was possible for the teachers and me to pick and choose, often during the first week of school, the children who would be successful or unsuccessful. Teachers used their influence to have successful-looking children assigned to their classrooms. Sad-looking children tended to be less successful. Happy children learned fast and were a joy to teach. They started out with an edge, as they tended to get the best teachers and be placed with the best-adjusted children.

There was a peculiarity about children who were going to be successful in school and a different peculiarity about children who were going to be failures. Also, parents of children who were going to be successful knew which teachers had the same peculiarity as their children. Parents used political influence to have their children placed with this successful-looking teacher. Our observations were rarely incorrect. To our shame we watched these children who were picked for failure traipse through elementary school, junior high and high school and into life as failures. Part of these children's failures could have been due to a self-fulfilling prophecy in that we predicted failure for them, expected failure, and allowed it to happen. Our only consolation was that we could say, "We told you so." We were good at picking failures but not very good at intervening. From my observation, things in schools remain much the same today.

Awareness of this fact bothered me and I prayed, "God, show me what this is that we see that makes us such great predictors of success and failure. God, help us to know how to intervene in this curse that we see in children."

God heard my prayer, but the answer to this question did not come easily. When the answer did come, others in my profession did not enthusiastically embrace it. The solution to the problem of intervention required, and still does, careful work on the part of those who are supposed to be professionals at intervention. I quickly learned that most often the only persons who cared about intervening to stop children from failure were parents. Chances are that if you do not arm yourself with the knowledge of when and how to intervene in the development and growth of your children, intervention will not occur. For this reason the Bible recommends parents bring up children in the way they should go. Schools, teachers, principals and ministers can help, but the main responsibility remains with parents.

Parents have an advantage over professionals when it comes to intervention. For professionals, intervention is extremely difficult, mainly, I think, because they make it such. They have to know a tremendous amount of information because of the fear of being wrongfully involved. All kinds of liabilities are connected to what they do. Parents, on the other hand, do not have to know all the researched facts before they can become positively involved with their children's emotional and mental growth. It is easier for parents armed with a little correct information to intervene in the emotional growth of children, than it is for professionals to intervene with massive amounts of knowledge.

Science is still looking for the causes of behavior, whereas the Gospel Model explains behavior fully. Many parents are conditioned to believe effective intervention cannot be easily done in a secure, inexpensive, and enjoyable way. Parents need to know that all that science and research tells about intervention is illustrated, exemplified, and described in the Bible. To see why and how behavior really occurs, behavior is best viewed through the Gospel Model. Raising children is the most natural thing parents do. God has given parents the innate knowledge of how to raise children and the proper instruction in the Scriptures. In using this innate knowledge, practice your faith in child rearing.

That the Bible explains behavior was very comforting to learn. After having done a tremendous amount of scientific and academic research, to find this knowledge had always been available was rewarding. Many parents were already using it although like my mother, they had not defined it as the Gospel Model. The defining of the Gospel Model to parents, who have been using it, helps them to see more clearly the correct path they are on in child rearing. The defining of the Gospel Model is a real epiphany.

As the years passed, parents kept coming to school with the haunting questions. "Why does my child fight so much with other children?" "How do I discipline my child?" "Why is my child not learning to read?" "Why is my child disrespectful to teachers?" "Why is it so difficult to get my child to go to school?" "Why is my teen stealing?"

We kept giving the old familiar answers to these troubled parents. "Make sure your child gets eight to ten hours of sleep each night." "Take him off sugar." "Provide her with a quiet place to study." "Limit the amount of TV he watches." "Read to your child."

Already you can see the irrationality in the above. We were the professionals. We knew best, but the reasons we gave for these children that were picked to fail, were not accurate. We knew it and the parents knew it. We all knew children were going to fail for other reasons than we alluded to with our patented and quick-fix answers. We knew that no matter what was told to these parents that their children were going to fail.

Professionals offer smug and simple answers and think they have done their duty. No wonder parents become angry with teachers and principals. If the answers to parents' questions were so easy to answer, why did they bother to ask? With most troubled children and parents, traditional answers do not work. Professionals, most of the time, blame the parents for the failure of children, pointing to dysfunctional families as the main causal relationship for failure of children. The term *dysfunctional* has become a catchall phrase to explain what is wrong when nobody really knows.

We looked everywhere in the literature for better answers. We attended conferences and seminars and listened to anybody who was supposed to be in the know about at-risk children. In prayer, the question asked was this: "What was the way or manner in which children should be raised to keep them from failure?"

The children identified for both failure and success in school came from all types of families: wealthy, indigent, intellectual, illiterate, professional, and upper class. As it turned out, the social and financial status of families did not have a lot to do with the ability of parents to intervene or of children to succeed. Therefore, the answer to the question was not to be found in the social culture of the child, but in something personal about the child that his parents and family provided to personality development.

Personality characteristics that led to success in school and the personality traits that led to failure were certainly before us for examination. The answer was so simple. Children needed to know who they were by what they did and to have a goal to work towards. Working with the children of Quick Success taught us the essential knowledge needed in using the Gospel Model. The Gospel Model created in parents a confident feeling in their ability to intervene in personality development of children. Parents learned to take charge in this area.

A review of how the Apostle Paul intervened in the development of his star pupil and son illustrates the successful raising of children as done in the Bible. Paul had chosen Timothy as his son and a child who was going to be successful. Paul writes a letter to Timothy, greeting him and checking on how his education was progressing. Timothy was the young pastor of the church of the Ephesians. First, the Apostle Paul reminds Timothy who his father in the Lord was and that he, Paul, had placed into Timothy the sound mind of Christ. Paul reminds Timothy of how this mind was in his grandmother and his mother and was now passed down to him. Notice that Paul wanted the sound mind of Christ to remain in Timothy and continue to carry him to adulthood (1 Timothy 1:1).

Paul considered himself to be Timothy's father. He points out to his son how powerful his life must be since he was raised within the pattern of the Gospel Model. Paul was sure that Timothy could fight off all the attacks of the devil, because he had the inner strength and the mind of God working in him. Timothy knew who he was, that he could change his environment, and knew what his goals were in life. He had learned to never give up. Paul continually viewed his son's growth through the Gospel Model and was always ready to correct Timothy's personality if the need ever arose.

Apostle Paul did to Timothy what the parents of the Quick Success children did for their children. They all used the Gospel Model to view their children's growth and development. Parents reinforced good behavior. When maladaptive qualities appeared, the parents knew how to intervene. Once the parents and school staff began working the model together, the history of intervention began to grow into something important.

CHAPTER FIVE

The Anatomy of the Gospel Model

Philippians 2:5: *Let this mind be in you, which was also in Christ Jesus.*

The body of Christ is greater than all its parts. We, on the other hand, are not mentally powerful enough to comprehend God's totality. By looking at the anatomy of the Gospel Model the part of God, which is doing something then, can be comprehended and seen. Only parts of God, which are shared with mankind, can be seen and explored. An understanding of the anatomy of the Gospel Model and its functioning is important, because it is the parents' duty to duplicate the model in children.

The next three chapters of this book are about the anatomy of the Gospel Model. In a very real sense the Gospel Model is like a human body, but it is more translucent to allow viewers to observe all the body systems working and performing together to make the body what it is. Indeed, the Gospel Model is the body of Christ and you are privileged to see how Jesus Christ operates in hearts of children and adults to create a lifestyle that directs persons to success rather than failure.

Functional Anatomy

Jesus Christ summarized the model several times. Once in John 3:16 when He announced, *For God so loved the world, that he gave his only begotten Son, that whosoever believeth in him should not perish, but have everlasting life.* This was the model in action. The goal or purpose was to save man. Sending the Son did this, which is what God did. God had an active faith that His Son could do the job. God is the Redeemer because he is saving us now. Without the doing, spiritual atrophy sets in, like in all bodies: no action, no model, no life.

Who You Are	What You Do	Purpose
Jesus Christ	Died For Us	Salvation
Savior	Saved and Healed	Man Restored
Better Speaker	Gestures, Forceful	Better Understood

The above is the summary of the model God wants His children to follow. Jesus' purpose was to save the world or society. To do so, He had to die for our sins. This act made Him the Savior. He was what He did. In the same manner, we are Christians because we live a Christian lifestyle. You are not what you say you are, you are what you do. God said to Moses, "I am that I do." God wants to be seen as a verb.

Christianity receives a bad image from Christians who are not willing to do God's will. That is why Christ indicated that those who were not for Him were against Him. Use the translucent body of Christ to duplicate Christ in the world. Everything we do is to be done within the model or image of Christ. In Isaiah 61:3, Jesus Christ is referred to as the "planting of the Lord" and in Isaiah 9:6, the Bible explains the image of Christ in terms of what He will do:

For unto us a child is born, unto us a son is given: and the govern-ment shall be upon his shoulder: and his name shall be called Won-derful, Counseller, The mighty God, The everlasting Father, The Prince of Peace.

Pastors and teachers are to use the image of Christ in all things. The Gospel Model can be followed to avoid conflicts within groups and to establish unity of purpose or to establish a plan of action for personal accomplishments. For example, the church educational committee wants to remodel three Sun-day school classrooms. Now with the stated goal, what must the committee do to see that the work is done? Whatever has to be done to accomplish the goal can be listed. People are needed to lay flooring tile, to paint, to clean windows, and to provide furniture. In going about their work these people are "being" a committee on education. The committee is what it does and does what it takes to accomplish its purpose.

A pastor has a goal to bring unity to a church. Such a church is perishing for the lack of making Christ work for them. He must first convince the membership of a common goal. The goal may be to establish the church's doings as the *Christian Asser-tive Effort*. By focusing on this goal, the membership will take on several tasks which will require cooperation. When the or-ganization of the programming is established and functioning as in Pastor John Doe's church, the church becomes what it does—a unified assertive church. The pastor becomes an asser-tive Christian, accomplishes his goal, and restores unity to the church. Unity is established as the church body focuses on one goal. God only makes an appearance in a church when there is unity of purpose. The better the body, the better its parts work together.

Unity was a gift found in the way the Hankins family worked out their differences on how children should be raised in Quick

Success Two. Agreement came with the selection of a strategy upon which both parents could agree. The differences they had were left out of the new strategy and unity of how to raise children was restored.

Rev. John Doe is using the above functional anatomy of the Gospel Model to improve his sermon presentations. He wants to become more demonstrative in his delivery. That is his stated goal. What must he do to be more demonstrative? He decided to remove a microphone attached to his lapel. He wanted to throw his voice to the last person in the last row of seats in the church. To help him project his voice more demonstratively he removes the microphone from his lapel. His gestures are somewhat more visible because he is gesturing to the whole congregation. He set his goal, he figured out what to do, and he became a more excellent speaker. What he did is what he became. This is an example of the Gospel Model in action. Using the Gospel Model is only limited to one's imagination.

In reading through the Bible, notice that all of God's great people followed this formula for success. Parents determined what characteristics they wanted placed in the lives of children, worked towards that end, and became outstanding parents. This is how the Gospel Model functions as a whole body. A person sets goals, does what is needed to change the situation, and becomes what he does.

What one sees when looking through the translucent Gospel Model are dynamic functions that can be compared to a machine, such as an automobile. Do car companies compete to build the best automobiles without using the best-engineered parts? When a car runs well, we know the parts are functioning the way the engineer designed the parts to function. Engineers must be accurate in their designs, for they know that one damaged part can shut down the whole car. This same analogy holds true with the relationship of raising children by the Gospel Model. It is important that the correctly engineered parts of the model be built into children.

The Gospel Model said, *Thou shalt love the Lord thy God with all thy heart, and with all thy soul, and with all thy strength, and with all thy mind; and thy neighbour as thyself* (Luke 10:27). These words referred to the anatomy of the model by listing its working parts. Love with the heart, soul, mind, and strength was what Jesus wanted to achieve in our lives with His example. Jesus is the Gospel Model. It remains for man to duplicate this model in order to be saved and to save children. Raise children by building the anatomy of the Gospel Model in children one part at a time.

In the previous chapter schoolteachers freely gave advice about how to educate children. Much of this advice was useless. What's wrong with my child? The answer should match the question with the purpose of building something in a child. It was not bad advice that the teachers offered the Hankins family but most all parents knew their children needed eight to ten hours of sleep each night. As it was, we did not offer advice that could be used to solve their problems. The Gospel Model does not discuss meaningless issues, but takes parents directly to the personality makeup of children where positive traits can be strengthened and negative traits can be eliminated.

GOALS and SINS: David, Absalom, and Sue (functional anatomy continued)

What are the components of the Gospel Model? The Gospel Model is a lifestyle when duplicated in the lives of children. The solutions to the children of Quick Success began by working with a single problem. William stopped learning, Matthew quit socializing, and Ryan seemed lost. But the solution to their problems was a cure that lasted for a lifetime.

If at any time a person stops for whatever reason from following the lifestyle of Christ, the door is open for the return of many developmental problems for children. In the following paragraphs, notice the serious problems King David created for himself and his family by vacillating back and forth between two styles of behavior which are called GOALS and SINS.

Two distinct styles of behavior appear in David's life and the lives of his children. The difference involves that peculiarity about children discussed earlier. God scripted the traits and characteristics of the people in the Bible and presented these for psychological study. Psychology is the study of both human and animal behavior; the best possible observations of man's behavior are biblical case studies. The people of God are expected to learn both God's and Satan's way and model from biblical observation.

Once parents are aware of the lifestyle that emanates from each model, an actual choice can be made to choose a style of living that leads to success or failure for children. The two life styles are GOALS and SINS.

GOALS stands for *God's Oriented Adaptable Life Style*. The traits of persons with GOALS are feelings of high self-esteem and worthiness, self-confidence, a will to complete tasks, respect for authority, sound reasoning, expectations of success, and righteous goals.

SINS stands for *Satan's Inadequate Naturalistic Style*. The traits of SINS are poor self-image, low self-esteem, tendencies to give up on difficult tasks, a rebellious and defiant attitude towards authority, dishonesty, a logic that answers to carnal desires, depression, and an unwillingness to cooperate with others. SINS will stop at nothing to get its way, even if it means disrupting the lifestyles of others. SINS does not place high values on the wants and needs of the group, but seeks the good for self and its own. In SINS is illustrated the lifestyles of humanist, naturalist, racial bigots, Nazis, KKK members, moral relativity, and disrespect for any Absolute authority such as God.

If David the shepherd boy were in your classroom, it would be easy to pick him as having the qualities to be the next king of Israel. David would obviously be a product of GOALS and a functional lifestyle that leads to success. David's son Absalom, if he were in the classroom, he would be identified as a rebellious child doomed for failure. It would be obvious that he was raised under the influence of SINS. Absalom rebelled against his father and almost split the nation of Israel in half. He had earlier killed his brother who had slept with his sister (2 Sam. 13:1). If you know the life story of King David, you are aware that his lifestyle was like SINS at the time he raised his children. At the end of his life David cried for his son Absalom who died an untimely death. But it was David's lifestyle that doomed Absalom.

Previously to the death of Absalom it was David's lifestyle of SINS that made him a poor father without a pure heart. Lifestyles of parents dictate what lifestyle is passed on to children. Children generally believe life should be lived the way their parents actually live.

Dr. Robert Coles is a professor of psychiatry at the Harvard Medical School and a Pulitzer Prize winning author of *The Spiritual Life of Children*. He insists in his book *The Moral Intelligence of Children*, it is valuable to teach children the Ten Commandments, the Golden Rule, and the moral sayings of Christ; but when it comes to children actually learning moral values, Coles says children learn these from the example of parents and adults. This would certainly be true in King David's children. In other words, Dr. Coles claims that children learn from what their parents actually do and not what they say. Children learn behavior from the lifestyles of their parents.

It will not be the single mistake you make in child rearing that will doom your children. It will be the lifestyle lived before children while they are developing. David learned this to be true but too late for some of his children. If parents want to teach their small ones high morals, they had better walk the walk as well as talk the talk. It is a fact that children need to observe parents and adults doing the right thing. Noah built the ark although it had never rained. He must have looked silly—yet he saved his children.

How about Sue? How did her mother save her? Some children are physically beautiful, face it! However, children who are courteous and behave well always seem to be pretty. Little girls form a better self-concept of beauty as they learn that beauty is as beauty does. Sue was a junior high student and wanted to be a cheerleader for the school basketball team. She, however, did not have the physique to do the stunts and jumps that cheerleading required. She went out for cheerleader and did not make the squad. She went to the coach of the basketball team and asked how she could support the team. The coach put her in charge of keeping the statistics of the basketball players' performances. Sue went a step further. She started a pep club to give support to the cheerleaders.

Already you can see that Sue had a great attitude and her lifestyle was something to admire. At the end of the school year, there was a banquet and dance to honor all the athletes in the school. The athletes were given the privilege to select a queen for the banquet and dance. Without exception the athletic queen had always been a cheerleader and one of the physically most beautiful girls in the school. This year was the exception. Sue was overwhelmingly selected the queen.

Her popularity was no accident. Sue's mother was one of the greatest ladies to ever live. Her lifestyle was that of GOALS. She instilled in her daughter the concept that you are what you do and if you want friends, you must be a friend. Actually, I have observed Sue for years. She appears to have been successful at everything she has attempted, including raising children. Today she is very slender and beautiful. Sue's mother embraced the model of GOALS. To teach what Dr. Coles referred to requires consistency. There are many examples like King David where parents have done the opposite.

GOALS and SINS: Operationally Defined Terms

All models seem to use operationally defined terms that make their explanations seem different. Bloom's Taxonomy uses *cognitive* and *affective* domains of behavior. These terms refer to whatever the model has defined these to mean. We also use operationally defined terms in describing the Gospel Model. The Gospel Model is an operationally defined term. It refers to its definition. It is what it says it is. It is Jesus Christ.

A child who has learned to live by this model knows who he is, what he can do to change the world, has goals and, intends to achieve. How strongly these three components are entrenched in the heart will determine whether a person has GOALS or SINS, two more operationally defined terms. Here is one more illustration where the two lifestyles can be observed.

Johnny and Larry were both in the fifth grade and possessed the same IQ scores of 100. Both were from middle class families and were neighbors. The fifth grade teacher gave the class an unannounced test of multiplication problems in math class. Both students failed the test and both were very much disappointed.

Larry explained to his parents why he failed the test. *My teacher does not like me. She surprised me with a test so I would make a bad grade. Besides, you know that I am not good at math. Math is hard. I am not as smart as the other children in math. The teacher does not like me and she is a bad person. Besides all this, I don't see any use in knowing about multiplication of numbers. I am not going to be a math-*

ematics expert or a doctor, or anything like that. I hate going to math class and I hate school.

Johnny explained to his parents why he failed the test. *The teacher was trying to show me that I needed to study my multiplication facts. She sure did get the message through to me. I was embarrassed. The next time I'll show her that I can do the work. I like the teacher and I want her to know that I am smart. I will just have to work harder to learn this math, especially if I want to be a doctor when I grow up. School is the place for me to learn these things that will help me later. I like school and can not wait to show the class what I know.*

When Johnny and Larry take the next test on multiplication facts, which one do you think will do the best? Which child is more like what you want your child to be? From when you were a child, can you identify with any characteristics that either Johnny or Larry had? Can you identify two ways of thinking and responding which will lead Johnny to succeed and Larry to fail? What you are seeing is the difference between two children that could allow you to predict which one would be successful in life and which one would be less successful.

These two lifestyles, GOALS and SINS, were being seen in school in the first grade that allowed teachers to be such great predictors of successful and unsuccessful children. Teachers were rarely wrong in their predictions about which children would be successful. The epiphany: it was a simple task of changing the way the children thought from SINS (a maladaptive way of thinking) to GOALS (an adaptable way of thinking). Ask the question, what must I do? The teachers who saw the value in changing the thinking process of children used stories and the careful ordering of their words in giving instructions to ease the children towards an adaptable way of responding and thinking. I personally made great use of the story of the Little

Red Train that thought it could, that thought it could and finally did. It did make it over the mountain. Quick Success I, II, and III remain excellent examples of the use of the Gospel Model. It was so easy to change the minds of William, Matthew and Ryan and thereby change their styles of living.

Several terms are operationally defined in explaining the anatomy of lifestyles. *Mindset* is a way of thinking that solicits an automatic response. *Structure* refers to how mindsets are connected to other mindsets to guide responses.

The *mind* is the largest grouping of mindsets and understandings. The *heart* is that part of the mind that interprets and determines what behavior will be like: if that behavior will be hedonistic in nature or altruistic in nature.

Intervention is the process and strategy used to change the mindsets, mind, and heart of children. *Immunization* is structuring the heart of a person so that person resists the bad effects of life events. Jesus taught that the bad came from the heart.

It is the complete man, to which the rich man said from his heart that he would tear down his barns and build greater. With his very being he listened to his evil, hedonistic heart. With his mind, the rich man could not understand that he was doing evil. What fault could there be in building bigger barns? The soul then directed the rich man's strength to carry out his new objective of building more and better barns (Luke 12:18).

In the parable of the rich man building better barns, we see the response to a tragic goal fulfillment, because he died and left all his wealth to others. Let us examine his lifestyle through the Gospel Model and compare it to the parable of the Good Samaritan with which most readers are already familiar and can relate (Luke 10:25–37).

I am	change things	goals.
Rich Man	Build better, bigger	
continued wealthy status		
Good Samaritan make world better by sharing		
heavenly wealth stored		

It is relatively simple to identify the lifestyle of the rich man as being SINS and the Good Samaritan's as being GOALS. Both the rich man and the Good Samaritan had wealth. Both wanted to lay up wealth for the future. Both men had a heart, but one heart was structured after the Gospel Model of GOALS, for this heart loved his fellow man. The heart of the Gospel Model—GOALS—sought for the good of all men and this became his heavenly reward. The rich man could have been like the Good Samaritan but his heart was different in that it convinced the soul and body to exert its will (strength) to worship the value of money. His heart produced evil just like Jesus said it would.

In a study of ethics a person who lives for pleasure is called a hedonist. An altruistic person is one who is generous and giving with his wealth, whatever this wealth might be. The Good Samaritan gave both of his time and money and has been a model for centuries in showing how people should live with neighbors.

The rich man was surprised in that he did not live long enough to enjoy having his wealth stored in new, bigger barns. Had the rich man been given a second chance, he most likely would have changed himself and his outcome. Changing goals changes outcomes. The rich man would need only to change one mindset to change from maladaptive to adaptive or from SINS to GOALS in order to change all other points in his life.

For example, to change his goal from selfishness to sharing would necessitate that he would have a different reaction to the needs of others, which would be in response to a different goal to share his wealth rather than store it up. The true meaning of *altruism* is that it is better to give. If the goal had changed for the rich man, his reaction would have changed. One can see clearly that the only way to save the rich man would have been to change his goals.

Do you see how important goals are in raising children? See how changing goals for children can be a valuable tool in intervention. Goal setting is an important part in the functional anatomy of the Gospel Model. Intervention would be to change the goals of at-risk children. What kind of parent do you think the rich man would have been? The rich man's goals did not include carrying for neighbors. In being truly altruistic, the Good Samaritan had a great advantage. He was immunized from the bad effects of wealth. Children who enter school without having learned to share receive a fate similar to that of the rich man. Children learn quickly to ignore selfish children. Style is everything.

A changed rich man would have a pure heart to guide him, having his old heart changed or cleansed by a new way of thinking. Evangelical Christians call this "being born again", which is for adults; but the Bible also says to bring children up in the nurture and admonition of the Lord (Ephesians 6:4). The point is that adults need to be converted because of association with a style of living that matches SINS. Having one's mind transformed is a religious conversion. In being born again, which is to become a new creature, involves replacing SINS with GOALS. Children are supposed to be raised in the nurture of this new mind. That is what happens to children when parents instill the proper mindsets in the heart of children, they are built up as a new and stronger person to live a lifestyle like GOALS and will most likely choose GOALS as a lifestyle at maturity.

It was too bad for the rich man. His parents did not find the time to build the Gospel Model in him. Childhood was the season for the rich man to learn to know God. Think what a better person the rich man would have been if his parents had raised him by the Gospel Model.

Mindsets: Part of the Anatomy of the Gospel Model

As adults we are free to choose the course of personality development and our way of thinking. We can choose Christianity as a way of thinking and direct our behavior towards the goal of being a Christian. Infants are not allowed this freedom of choice but are subject to respond to their environment and to learn within their immediate surroundings. An advantage adults have over infants is that adults are mature enough to know the difference between good and evil; they are mentally ready to practice the discriminatory powers of the mind. Parents mostly choose the experiences children have.

This can be a disadvantage when adults carry over from their childhood the memory of bad experiences with which to reason and think. These bad memories become flaws in the adult thinking process. An example of a flawed memory is that of a woman abused by her father during childhood. As an adult she thinks adult men are something to be feared. When it comes to men, she may not want to choose a male for a mate. She could choose any variety of lifestyles to avoid becoming involved with a male.

Already you can see problems for the children that this woman might parent. Would she be able to teach children the things necessary to help them adjust to the opposite sex? Infants are just beginning to respond to stimuli and can be easily guided as they learn to think. If infants have Christian parents, they have a great advantage in that their initial experiences will have fewer flaws or bad mindsets. As they approach adulthood they will have been exposed to fewer negative experiences.

Too many experiences too soon cloud the issues of important facts. Many people enjoy working picture puzzles. The more pieces to a puzzle the greater the challenge to put all the pieces in the correct place. The first step in working a puzzle is to find the four corner pieces, then the remaining border pieces, and then fill in the inner portions and spaces. If you do not build a frame or border first, it is thousands of times more difficult to solve the puzzle. Too many experiences make learning for adults and children more difficult without first having a structure, that is, corner and border pieces, that makes all the remaining pieces clearly more meaningful—thus the Gospel Model.

To properly make use of the numerous experiences that children have, the frame of reference becomes important. Experiences are the pieces of the puzzle of life. The danger with children is that they are often forced to put things together before the structure is built. By using the Gospel Model, parents can give guidance and direction to children by providing an adequate frame of reference called mindsets. Good mindsets equal GOALS. Poor mindsets equal SINS.

The Gospel Model has corner pieces and borders called mindsets. Mindsets are formed by early experiences. A woman abused by her father forms a mindset of men. Had her father been a Christian, can you see how her life would have been different? If you can see and understand how she would have been different, you are beginning to view life through the Gospel Model. You know some facts about her as an abused child without ever having met her. You can surmise from her frame of reference how her life might have been different had the Gospel Model been a part of her early experiences.

Most adults have already made up their minds of how they view life, making it more difficult for them to see and discover God's plan for them, especially if they have a lifestyle like SINS. It is unusual for any new convert to Christianity in America to not have preconceived ideas handed down to them from the Baptist, Methodist, Catholic, Presbyterians, Pentecostals, and others, although most all agree that part of religious conversion involves the re-assessment of values. God intervenes in the adult lifestyle to create a new type of thinking.

Most of the above religious beliefs do not take the act of raising children into consideration when they announce the religious concepts that make them different from the rest of society. This suggests that Christianity, as a whole, has not thought enough or adequately on the subject of raising children.

Infants as they begin to learn have no competition with previous learning. This is the time parents need to be familiar with how to build mindsets. Since parents have a free reign to teach their children the values of the household, children will learn for the most part what parents allow and teach. For parents, the secret is to know early on how they want their children to think and then teach that way of thinking. This is where the value of mindsets within the Gospel Model becomes extremely important. There are mindsets that parents do not want their children to know, like the above-mentioned abused woman.

When God tries to enlighten new Christians on how to raise children, God competes with a lot of different ideas that people have already accepted as functional. The Bible refers to these ideas which conflict with what God wants us to know as strongholds (2 Corinthians 10:4). These strongholds limit the spiritual growth of God's children. The strongholds which infants have are acquired from parents through incorrect mindsets established by what children are initially allowed to learn. Incorrect thinking learned early in life can haunt a child all the way through adulthood.

First-learned mindsets guide a child's emotional development into adulthood. For example, what do you think the child abused by her father thought of men when she became a woman? The closest term in child psychology to *stronghold* is a bad *mindset*. A *mindset* is a point of view that a person has which solicits an automatic response.

For example, in Africa the word *cat* might solicit a very negative emotional response by association with an animal that could eat a person. In the U.S.A. it is common for little children to play with cats and enjoy the play. As you can see, many words and experiences are viewed in different ways depending on the mindset.

Different cultures have different mindsets, which makes each culture unique. An example of a national mindset is how the people of the People's Republic of China think and feel about saving face. Saving face is more important to them than life. Americans do not like to be dishonored; but in diplomatic conflicts the United States has been willing to apologize to China, although the United States had done no wrong. The greater value for life was invoked in order to protect the well being of American citizens who were held captive by the People's Republic of China. The mindset of the U.S.A. involved the value of individual safety above that of saving face. If mindsets are powerful enough to direct the behavior of great nations, think of the wonderful power that is placed in the lives of children who learn to think with the mindsets of God and the Gospel Model.

In the matter of child rearing, we are interested in establishing automatic responses in children that reflect our Christian values. These would be good mindsets (GOALS) as opposed to bad mindsets (SINS) that conflict with what God wants us to know. We are interested in bringing up children in the manner that promotes the Christian culture in children. We believe that a baby raised as God wants has a better chance of being successful in life. Therefore, we need to discover the mindsets that Christian children need to be taught, meaning parents are picking a type of personality for children to learn.

Goals Determine Lifestyles

Parents determine how a child will think and therefore, what a child will be as an adult. Parents can establish a clear view of how to create the personality of children from before birth. If parents have a goal in mind about personality and work towards training a child in that direction, the Gospel Model will provide parents with guidance in that direction.

Goals are a big part of the anatomy of the Gospel Model. Remember how we said appropriate goals could have saved the rich man. A key word in this instruction is *appropriate*. Common sense tells us that every child will not become the president of the U.S. The U.S. Army has selected a goal that every person should be "the best they can be" by joining the army. The army wants recruits to think of being successful by creating a mindset linking the army with success. Parents want to create a personality in children that dictates children will succeed in life regardless of the vocation they choose.

Parental goal setting for children should be aimed at making children successful regardless of the vocation they choose. Most parents would like to raise well-adjusted, normal children who are able to earn a living as adults, succeed in school, be reasonably popular, and have the proper social values. Christian parents typically want their children to love God, attend church, and pass on the family's value system to other generations.

Choose success as a goal. If a child is to be president, make him a successful president. Whatever he is, make him successful. It is too lofty of a goal to want children to be perfect like God or to be more than they can be. This caused all the problems in the beginning when Lucifer tried to be like God. Adam and Eve were trying to be like the gods when they ate of the tree of knowledge of good and evil.

There will be no perfect children or perfect parents. Discover what God wants a person's personality to be like and choose to develop children in that very reasonable direction. They can think their way to success. The direction and manner in which children develop will be determined by the *mindsets* available to them in their growing memory of experiences.

Do not give up on the Gospel Model of GOALS in directing the life of children, if the children turn out to be less than perfect as adults. Very few of the great men of God in the Bible were perfect. Some of the most noteworthy ones had great personality flaws and succumbed at times to SINS. However, the power of GOALS is strong and even if a child departs from the *way* as an adult, there is a tremendous chance that GOALS will end up taking control of this person's behavior. Having initially been trained by the Gospel Model allows a wayward child to return to its up bringing. That, at least, is God's promise.

CHAPTER SIX

Looking for the Mind

Anatomy of the Scientific Mind

In our first course of general psychology at the university, the professor asked the class, "What is psychology?"

A very intellectual looking student replied, "It is the study of the mind."

How incorrect he was and the professor, intending to get this one point across to the whole class, shouted, "No, we don't even know that there is a mind! If there is such a thing nobody has ever seen it, weighed it, taken a picture of it, or found it in an autopsy. So how can you study something unless you can see it?"

This is when I first learned about operationally defined terms. That is what the mind is, an operationally defined thing. It is true that our class had never seen a mind. But we all knew we had one. And, we knew that the campus counselor was always ready to psychoanalyze us using as a model the *id*, the *ego*, and *superego*, which were thought to be the three divisions of the mind according to Sigmund Freud.

The professor then told us kindly that psychology was the study of human and animal behavior. That was what psychology was, studying behavior. But who studies the mind? Did not psychologists do this? Psychologists define what the mind is, since not being able to find one in reality to weigh or take a picture of it. The mind was operationally defined as being what it did; it was a group of mental processes housed in the brain. Psychologist observes behavior and deduced what the state of the mind was that produced that behavior. By studying behavior the psychologist attempted to deduce the thought processes that were going on in one's brain.

Here is an example of novice students psychoanalyzing the mind. A student held his chest back, answered tough questions accurately in class, believed he knew everything, boasted about how smart he was, and the rest of us concluded that he had a big *ego*—the I or self. We did not always care for students who had big *egos*. We psychoanalyzed him and determined that he had a mind that thought too highly of self. His *id* had no decorum. His conscious, *superego*, had no pride. It did not bother us. We ignored him.

We were amateurs at analyzing minds but we could not resist. We used what was currently being studied, the psychoanalytic approach of Sigmund Freud, which stressed that events and experiences in childhood had a profound effect on the adult mind and behavior. Our analysis suggested to us that our fellow student had a bad childhood, was not properly toilet trained, had not been breast fed, and had been rejected by his peers at day care. What kind of mind did he have as a result of all this? Funny? Maybe! But we did what psychologists were doing; we studied behaviors to determine what was wrong with the mind of this young man.

We did with our limited knowledge what men have been doing since the beginning of time. People daily use psychoanalysis on each other but use a frame of reference logged by experiences in their own thought processes. They deduce continually from the behavior of others what others are thinking. In this way people evaluate others and assign them a social and mental status. Some people we like and some people we do not like. Some we think are smart and others, not.

The psychoanalytic model is just one approach among many used by science to examine the mind. People may not be familiar with any of the terminology of the models science uses, such as *ego, superego* and *id*. Yet, you can be sure that there is a frame of reference, a type of model, a definition of the mind that people use to evaluate others even if they cannot define it. When we examine ourselves or the mental development of our children, this important task of determining what the mind of children is like deserves a better structured approach than our common experiences provides for us. *In all thy ways acknowledge him, and he shall direct thy paths* (Proverbs 3:6). Christians must use Christ the Gospel Model to interpret behavior. This is really the only safe scientific way to evaluate how children are thinking.

The Biblical Mind

The Bible speaks often of the mind of God. Originally the mind of God was the same as man's mind. We are all familiar with how man's mind became corrupt and disordered. Twice God gave up on the perverted mind of man. God drove Adam and Eve from the Garden of Eden and sent the flood to destroy the mind of Noah's generation. These were the times that God rejected man's mind. All this because man's mind failed to be like God's mind which created man in God's image.

Throughout the Bible, prophets, poets and philosophers were curious about the mind as handed down to man by God. Is God a mind to be worshipped (John 1:1)? Here the Greek word *logo is* interpreted to mean Mind, Word, or God. Some readers of the Bible have lost much of the Jewish meaning of the mind as a process of doing things, such as creating. That God's thinking creates, there can be no doubt. God thought of the plan of salvation before it was completed in reality. One good thing about understanding the pattern of God's thinking in the Bible is that psychology of the biblical mind and creditable scientific psychology support each other.

The apostle Paul gathered his information from the main source. Jesus Christ educated Paul personally with visions and revelations as explained in the Second Epistle to the Corinthians (chapter 12). Other apostles had similar educational experiences such as John's famous revelation of Christ while on the island of Patmos. Here Jesus Christ communicated directly to John the revelation of God's Being. The New Testament writers also gathered their authority from the *thus saith the Lord* of the Old Testament, Jesus Christ and science. All three agree that the mind is created in men and children and that God is in a constant process of thinking of us.

Ephesians 6:4, *And, ye fathers, provoke not your children to wrath: but bring them up in the nurture and admonition of the Lord* is Paul explaining how to raise a child to have a structured mind that is automatically responding to the way of God. The two words *nurture* and *admonition* actually mean to bring children's thoughts through a structure like a house or household. The underlying meaning of *nurture and admonition* goes deeper in that it includes the meaning of household. That is like saying one learns to think comparable to the family tradition that structured the same thoughts of Abraham, Moses, and Jesus, the real family of God.

Jews think of themselves as members of the household of Abraham. As a people they have characteristics that they hold in common that defines them as Jews. If you are a member of a particular family, as you mature you take on the characteristics of the members of the household due to the close affiliation with the family. Families tend to talk alike, think alike, and even dress alike. You might say every family has an identifiable style.

The Christian is very much a part of the household of God with GOALS as his lifestyle. Therefore, in Philippians 2:5 Paul says: *Let this mind be in you, which was also in Christ Jesus.* The point here is that Paul wants fathers and mothers to build the mind of Christ in children—you can do this. And, the result will be to fulfill Proverbs 23:7: *For as he thinketh in his heart, so is he.*

Notice a very important distinction. It is not what a person thinks but *how* he thinks that creates and builds the mind. Both science and the Bible agree on this. Science today conducts extensive research to find out how specific minds think. Criminology and penology study the criminal mind with the hope that something can be learned to limit the effects of crime in our society. Social scientists are interested in identifying how different cultures and nationalities think so as to allow the government's diplomatic core to better deal with other countries. The child psychologist wants to know how children think at various stages of growth to guide children to make a better adjustment to their surroundings.

The apostle Paul did an in-depth study of both the Christian mind and the unbeliever's mind to ensure that he could instruct Christian parents how to chart a successful path leading to a Christian mind. What Paul identified for parents was the thinking structure of Jesus Christ. This is the mind that should be built in children and is the meaning of Ephesians 6:4.

Along with Jesus Christ, Paul taught the structure of the mind was like a house and part of a household. This is too evident to be debated. Jesus said that a person, who heard His sayings and did them, was like a wise man that built his house or mind on a rock and was able to withstand the storms of life. Parents are to use the sayings of Christ as a blueprint by which to train children; therefore, the building of a structured mind was building a lifestyle that would stand firmly. Such a house will be there after the rain, flood, and wind. The structured mind that was not built on the sayings of Christ would fall because it was not built on a firm foundation (Matthew 7:24). I like Luke's quote, the man *digged deep* and *laid the foundation.* The implication was that no matter how vehemently the streams of life events beat upon a mind established to follow God, it would not be shaken (Luke 6:48).

The man dug deep and laid a foundation on rock. That is what parents can do for children. Children and parents both, together, within the family, need to build their mindsets on a rock. Parents can completely build *the way* of thinking in the minds of children so they will be able to adapt better to life events. Children can know who they are, what they can do, and have goals. These mindsets are completely necessary to following the sayings of Christ.

Jesus cites another example of a man who was very happy to begin construction of a building, a tower for his family's protection. From the tower it would be possible to see his enemies afar off. He began a good thing. The tower was a tool to protect his household. From such a tower, the man could tell who was coming and determine what type of threat was approaching. Things then could be done to protect his household. But he did not finish the tower and his enemies began to make fun of him. Jesus said this man should have counted the cost of building before beginning (Luke 14:29).

It is a bad testimony when parents begin to raise their children in the admonition of Christianity and the children turn out to be terrible failures. We are not saying that every Christian family will turn out perfect children. But you would think that if the Christian's claim to having a superior lifestyle was true, there would be a higher incidence of successful children among Christians than among those who have a different lifestyle. We have not found any studies in child psychology or social science that definitively claimed any one particular religious belief, such as Christianity, had any special advantage for raising successful children.

It appears to me that the reason children of the Christian faith have no better advantage at succeeding in life over other children is that Christians do not use the Gospel Model of raising children any more often than the rest of society. However, we know that within Christianity there is a superior way to raise children so they will have a higher than normal incidence of success. Could it be that Christians are so tied to worldly ways of thinking, customs, and styles of living that they have not done the *sayings* of Christ? If this is the case, Christians need to do a better job of discovering and doing *the way*.

A model for teaching children to be successful at a higher incidence than normal has been found in scientific research and has always been in the Bible. It is the model that God used with the children of Israel in creating the great personalities of men and women of the Scriptures. Where, you say? It is the model we are talking about. The key is to use the correct model whether you find it in science or in the Bible.

The Carnal Mind

Paul often referred to the *mind of Christ* and the *carnal mind*, which is either adaptable or maladaptive in creating a lifestyle. The carnal mind seems very much like a cluster of maladaptive mindsets. The carnal mind is described throughout the New Testament with fairly strong slogans. In Acts 14:2 the Bible speaks of minds that were evil affected. In Romans 1:28 a reprobate mind is mentioned. Romans 8:7 identifies the carnal mind to be the enemy of God. Blinded minds, which avoided recognizing the truth, were recorded in 2 Corinthians 3:14. The Bible warns of a fleshly mind in Colossians 2:18. The same defiled mind that

Jesus talked about in the four gospels, Paul refers to in Titus 1:15. And James in James 1:8 spoke of a double-minded man being unstable in his ways. The description of the carnal mind does not exactly match the vocabulary of the various scientific models, but I do not believe any parent sees any value in teaching children this type of mind.

In 1 Corinthians 2:16, Paul says, *we have the mind of Christ.* What is this mind like? Paul says in Romans 7:25b, *with the mind I myself serve the law of God.* This is the same law that Paul identified from the Old Testament in Hebrews 8:10b, *I will put my laws into their mind, and write them in their hearts: and I will be to them a God.* This is evidence that the Bible teaches parents to teach children from a biblical model. It is no wonder that Paul said in Romans 8:6, *For to be carnally minded is death; but to be spiritually minded is life and peace.* Paul knew that a double-minded child was a terrible thing. Paul instructed his children in Romans 12:2: to *prove what is that good, and acceptable, and perfect, will of God* by transforming the mind. Peter saw the immunization power of the mind of Christ in children and adults when he said in 1 Peter 4:1, *arm yourselves likewise with the same mind.* Surely the Scripture supports the mind of Christ as a model for an adaptable way of thinking and the carnal mind as something to be cleansed.

It is important to continue to create the mind of Christ in children. The minds of children are like the kingdom of heaven. To continue to teach a child by the Gospel Model is to continue to build on what God already started. Contrary to popular belief, the Bible does not teach that children are born with a sinful heart. A child's heart is like God's heart. John's Gospel, chapter one, points out that Jesus lights the heart of every person who enters the world.

Logic teaches that Satan will go to work immediately to attempt to impose his lifestyle on children. But Satan will do this by first confusing parents as to what is the correct way to raise children. Satan will never admit that parents can do the job better than somebody else. God, however, expects parents to do the job. Children are born going the correct way. Bring them up in that way and not in the path of a carnal mind.

CHAPTER SEVEN

The Heart: The Structure of the Mind

Examine yourselves, whether ye be in the faith; prove your own selves. Know ye not your own selves. (2 Corinthians 13:5)

Examine was the concept that Jesus and Paul used for psychoanalysis. Chapters 7 and 8 of the Gospel according to John, is full of examples of Jesus making searching statements which caused the Pharisees to examine themselves to see if they were the ones without sin. More will be said about self-examination using a three-step method in a future chapter but do not refuse to understand that the Light of the world searches hearts for the purpose of showing us our faulty nature. Through the examination of psychological behavior, parents can determine the flawed characteristics that need to be purged from children's hearts and minds. Characteristics can be built into the mind to guarantee future growth within the frame of reference of the Gospel Model.

Jesus and Paul suggested a method of analysis that is the same as doctors and therapists use today. Jesus many times encouraged people to ask for that which they were seeking and often Jesus asked penetrating questions that forced people to look within their hearts for answers. By observing the response to examination Jesus always knew what people were thinking (Matthew 5:46 and 47, 6:25, 12:7, 19:16 12:7; Mark 14:36, 15:14 and more than 200 more references). Among all the references that cite the use of psychology by Jesus, the Scripture verses that contain the word *perceive* best express how Jesus used the science of psychology to reason about what was in peoples' hearts (Matthew 13:14, 22:18 ; Mark 2:8, 4:12, 8:17; Luke 5:22, 6:41, 9:47, 20:23; John 6:15). *Examine, perceive, discern* are just a few of the key words that demonstrate that Jesus and the disciples were viewing the mind by observing behavior which are the parts of the mental condition of the mind.

It is the same thing psychiatrists do when they ask patients to tell them about bad experiences they had as children. The psychiatrist is looking for those bad mindsets that have infiltrated into a person's sub-consciousness.

The examination of the minds of children is like the visualization of holding up to the window the Gospel Model and holding up to the window the way children are behaving. Compare behavior to the model. The difference between the Gospel Model and the way children actually think is the measure of the children's thinking that needs intervention.

In Quick Successes, William was not psychologically ready to adapt to the advanced learning level required in sixth grade. This was a characteristic of SINS. His opinion of himself was low, as he believed he was not very smart. He had no plans to improve and did not like himself or see himself as being capable. He had few if any stated goals. William had come to think that schoolwork was too difficult for him. William did not do well in school; therefore, he was what he did: not well, not smart, and had no purpose.

Several areas were corrected in William's psychology. One, William was shown that he was intelligent by learning to complete tasks. Two, William could change the difficulty of schoolwork by doing the schoolwork; and three, William set a goal of making all "A" grades very soon. By strategically changing SINS to GOALS, tremendous improvements were made in William's lifestyle. See how we examined William's mind.

If the Gospel Model of GOALS is present in children, fine. But, in areas where the pattern of goal setting, changing, and becoming is not found, some correcting or intervention is needed in the way children think. The closer children come to matching the GOALS pattern, the better they fit together in the body of Christ and the closer they are to having a structured personality that solicits success. The success pattern referred to is GOALS: *God's Oriented Adaptable Life Style*. That is the pattern we want children to have. A flawed personality equals SINS, which is *Satan's Inadequate Naturalistic Style*. Parents need to take steps to avoid teaching SINS to children.

Throughout the Bible when God wants to know what is in the mind of His children, He examines or searches the heart. The heart is the place from which both success and failure come. That is why David prayed:

> *Search me, O God, and know my heart: try me, and know my thoughts: And see if there be any wicked way in me, and lead me in the way everlasting.* (Psalm 139:23)

The *heart, the way, structure, mindsets, and maladaptive and adaptive explanatory lifestyles* are all one and the same and it is these that make up what Jesus called the heart. Again, Jesus pointed out that both good and evil came from the heart.

> *A good man out of the good treasure of the heart bringeth forth good things: and an evil man out of the evil treasure bringeth forth evil things.* (Matthew 12:35)

When Jesus spoke of a tree bringing forth both good and corrupt fruit, I believe He was talking about the heart of children. The result that children receive is a product of the frame from which their fruit originates. Jesus is saying that if you grow a good tree, you will have plenty of success. The Jews were the people of God and should have been God's fruit to spiritually feed the world. The tree was cursed because there was no fruit. Raise children in the following way. Grow a good tree and build a good heart and successful fruit will follow. It is a promise from God.

Even so every good tree bringeth forth good fruit; but a corrupt tree bringeth forth evil fruit. A good tree cannot bring forth evil fruit, neither can a corrupt tree bring forth good fruit. Every tree that bringeth not forth good fruit is hewn down, and cast into the fire. (Matthew 7:17–19)

The heart to Jesus was also like a filter that was put in the mind and was used to sort out flawed learning. The mind is a cluster of mental processes and thoughts that flows through the structure in the heart. A mindset formed by SINS brings a different response than a mindset formed by GOALS. If the heart is formed by SINS, it acts as a filter to take away the good. It is a GOALS heart that filters out evil.

Let us think about this for a minute. This explanation is really simple. A neat relationship exists between the heart and the mind. The heart is in the mind and is both controlled by the mind and has control over the mind. The best way to control the mind is to change the heart. The best way to change the heart is to change your mind. There is interdependence here; a manufacturing process goes on in the mind. The heart acts like a mold of a statue. The substances of the heart are thoughts and beliefs, which are like the clay or plaster that is poured in the mold. After setting in the mold for a while, the statue is removed from the mold. If you have a perfect mold, you retrieve a perfect statue. Having created a perfect statue, you may want to duplicate this perfection again and again. That is how the heart works; if it is perfect, it produces perfect thoughts and good behavior. If the heart is not pure, as King David prayed it would be, the behavior will be flawed.

The point is, if the mold has a flaw in it, the mold will always turn out imperfect statues. Children are like this. Their hearts, feelings, mindsets, and lifestyle mold them. Parents can determine the mold or model, that is, whether the mold will be SINS or GOALS. Parents can intervene when children do not reflect the perfect molding of the Gospel Model, which is GOALS. To allow SINS to dominate children, all parents must do is to do nothing.

In the Gospel Model of GOALS, the way, heart, lifestyle, or mindsets of a Christian consist of three basic beliefs. (1) A Christian believes that he is what he is because of an active faith: you are what you do. (2) A Christian believes there is a cause and effect relationship between himself and the world. (3) A Christian believes the outcomes in life can be determined, planed and achieved—in other words, goals are obtainable. It is this heart which parents have to instill in their children, which will result in structuring a lifestyle that automatically produces success or failure.

SINS is just the opposite of the Christian heart. Satan wants children to learn a way that causes destruction. Jealousy, resentment, and a follower's mentality with a belief that the world never changes and has no significant purpose, is SINS. The rich man tried and tested Satan's inadequate lifestyle and was left with nothing. A person who believes he is of value, based on what he has, who believes change will not occur, and who really does not care who suffers as long as he gets what he wants, this person suffers from an evil heart.

Raising Children in Households

We have discussed bringing children up in the nurture and admonition of the Lord. Jesus Christ and Paul viewed the mind as a house, which housed the thought processes that led individuals to either a successful or unsuccessful behavior. Jesus had a lot to say about the mind and wanted people to love God with their entire mind (Mark 12:30). He did miracles to put them back in their right mind (Mark 5:15). The type of miracles discussed in Quick Success and those in Pastor Doe's church are the real miracles that Jesus said His followers would do that would be greater than His. The miracle that Jesus performed on the mind was to change the heart—the deepest structured place in the mind that determines behavior.

In Matthew 15:18–19 Jesus made it clear that the things that came from within the heart defiled people. Defilement came from the heart which means that SINS is at the heart of the problem of children who are failing in life. According to this verse, the bad traits that came from an unclean heart or house were evil thoughts, spite and resentment, sexual misconduct, untruthfulness, and bad language, all the things we do not want children to learn. Can there be any doubt that Jesus was referring to the household of Satan?

In reviewing this particular verse, the description of an evil heart is very much like the description of an emotional illness called *conduct disorder* found in children and adolescents and often described in medical books and journals. The terminology of Jesus was different from our modern medical terminology. But, what Jesus called the heart, psychology calls mindsets.

Agreed, mindsets are beliefs that automatically solicit emotional and cognitive responses. Jesus points out that from the heart, a household of automatic responses, comes good or evil. It is the evil things that created a defiled mind. Do you see the difference between the household of God and the household of Satan? Do you see how parents create minds for God or for Satan?

Jesus said, *Blessed are the pure in heart: for they shall see God* (Matthew 5:8). It is sad that some children will never see God because they are not introduced to the power of the Gospel Model. At-risk children need to be put into a right mind, so they too automatically respond to have success. Do you see how raising children according to GOALS is called the blessing in the Bible?

In Matthew 12:43–45 Jesus tells a story of a demon that walked about looking for a place to rest and does not find it. This demon had come from a house. In fact, the demon had come from deep in the house, the heart of a man.

Then he saith, I will return into my house from whence I came out; and when he is come, he findeth it empty, swept, and garnished.

Then goeth he, and taketh with himself seven other spirits more wicked than himself, and they enter in and dwell there: and the last state of that man is worse than the first.

To Jesus the house was the mind and heart. From this story, it is clear that Jesus understood the progression of the growth of evil demons in the character of modern day youth. Conduct and opposition disorders do spring up as children learn bad behavior. The bad behavior is called criminal when continued as an adult and as the behavior becomes more nauseous, it requires a response from society.

Let us review again Ephesians 6:4, *And, ye fathers, provoke not your children to wrath: but bring them up in the nurture and admonition of the Lord.* The Greek word that means nurture in English also means *structure* in both English and Greek, like a house is structured or framed up. Paul was interested in structuring the mind of children so as to have children able to automatically respond to life events with an active faith. In this structured mind, Paul saw specific sections or areas of thoughts that are built. (See Matthew 7:26–27; 10:6; 12:44; 23:38; John 14:1–4).

When children have developed a behavior pattern, called a syndrome in psychology, which responds resiliently and positively to life events, they are reacting from a heart structured by God. Behavior patterns cause children to misbehave and points to the building of an evil heart.

Acts 7:21: *And when he was cast out, Pharaoh's daughter took him up, and nourished him for her own son.* This child was Moses. In the second chapter of Exodus is the story of where Moses' mother was called to nurse her own child that became the child of Pharaoh's daughter. Can there be any doubt that the one who nursed Moses also helped structure his mind and heart?

Verse 22, *And Moses was learned in all the wisdom of the Egyptians, and was mighty in words and in deeds.* But in verse 23, Moses considered the Hebrews to be his brothers because it was in his heart to be with them. *And when he was full forty years old, it came into his heart to visit his brethren the children of Israel.* Indeed, his actions came from a structured mind from his true heart. Moses knew who he was and acted accordingly. He adopted the goal to free the Hebrews by the way handed down to him from his real mother. Moses knew he was of the household of Israel. Moses' walk with God is an example of the Gospel Model of child rearing. The first and most important ingredient of raising a child is to teach the child of whose household he is.

Moses was a wise man that God chose to help a nation to conform to the model or image of God. God could choose Moses because his mother prepared him to be chosen. Moses' real mother was always there for him in that she had structured his mind and built his household to respond to God, and thereby exercised power over the behavior of Moses. Parents today can always be in the minds of children to influence their behavior. Parents clearly can structure the minds of children for success and not failure. The heart can protect them from the effects of potentially harmful experiences as they mature. It is really so very simple. This explains why Moses thought of himself as a Hebrew although he was raised in the household of Egypt.

Everything Moses learned from his experiences in life he learned through the structured mind or heart that his mother had built for him. He learned from the background that he knew who he was, a Hebrew child. He believed he could change things for himself and his people, which is the second most important ingredient in the structure of God. He was attempting to free his people when he first killed the Egyptian who was abusing his Hebrew brother.

The change in the Hebrew's world did not take place then, but Moses would keep trying to reach his goal until his people were set free forty years later. When a child knows he can make things different, he keeps trying and is much less likely to give up.

Forty years later, through the Gospel Model's structured mind, Moses was ready to continue following God's *way* down to the very place on the map where the children of Israel were to leave Egypt. Moses had adopted a goal to be achieved, which is the third most important ingredient to the structured mind of God.

> And it came to pass, when Pharaoh had let the people go, that God led them not through the way of the land of the Philistines, although that was near; for God said, Lest peradventure the people repent when they see war, and they return to Egypt. (Exodus 13:17)

God commanded Moses not to bring the children out through the *way* of the Philistines, although it was the most direct route, because battle with the Philistines might discourage the children too much too soon in their learning to travel *the way*. Do not pressure children too much. Lead them by making them want to follow you. Performance will come naturally when the structure of the Gospel Model is put in place. Just keep talking to children and the Word of God will be sown in their hearts. Parents start building from the foundation and must wait to put the roof on. Don't rush it.

How much of a challenge to a child is too much? When Moses was forty years old, he attempted to deliver the Hebrews from captivity. That was too soon. But, he was on his *way*. He failed at his initial attempt to be a leader. But he was on his *way* to become a redeemer.

Moses was eighty years old, yet the structure—the concept of the *way*, the heart of a Hebrew—which his mother taught him as a child, never failed him. It kept him on the *way* and in the household. Moses responded to God for over one hundred years, using what his parents instilled in him. He became one of the greatest religious leaders of all time. When his time came, he was ready to respond.

One important item needs to be re-emphasized. Moses' mother only taught her son the structure of the mind of a Hebrew. That was enough. He learned most other things from the house of Pharaoh; as Scripture indicates, he was learned in all the ways and wisdom of the Egyptians. Parents cannot be versed in all the knowledge in the world on how to raise children. But from the time Moses was an infant, the Hebrew mother owned his heart. Moses looked at all he learned from the Egyptians through the Gospel Model. You can count on this fact: most of the information learned by children will be from the world. The model made the difference in Moses' life and it can for your children too. Children will know what path to take in life if we give them a pure heart.

The Helping Hand of the Heart

Moses led the children of Israel through the Red Sea the easy way. God split the sea for them and once the children of God crossed the Red Sea, God the Father arranged several crisis events and obstacles with which to teach them to overcome hardship and to overcome a certain amount of failure. This was therapeutic suffering.

Often the children of Israel thought they were in danger. But God's protective hand was there. If parents structure their children today, they too will see God's protective hand in their children's lives all the way to adulthood. Parents today can find the protective hand of God in child rearing and can raise children comfortably. This is the protective hand that rides the school bus with your child.

I have seen children in department stores with their mothers who knew their child would run off, get lost, and suffer trauma from being lost. To avoid this, a few parents resorted to harnesses to restrain the movement of their children. Harnesses did allow children a certain amount of freedom to move about but only as far as the leash on the harness would allow. Children brought up in the *way* have a harness on them to pull them back into the *way*. Once children are headed in the correct direction, it is not easy for them to become lost. God went with the children of Israel and led them by a fire by night and a cloud by day (Exodus 13:21). He went with them harnessed out of Egypt. This is exactly how the Gospel Model works on children (Exodus 13:18).

Helping Hand of the Church

Moses was a great leader but not by himself. He had to have help. He had to learn to use the abilities of others to direct his children. Very few people are able to build a house without assistance from others. Dating back to Moses the Bible clearly teaches that the church is to assist young adults in teaching children. For example, Moses adopted a method provided by his father-in-law to teach the children of Israel the commandments and laws of God. Moses' father-in-law counseled Moses with these paraphrased words from Exodus 18:13–20.

> *Don't set here alone by yourself, Moses, to judge Israel. This is not a good thing to do as you are killing yourself. Train others to make decisions on the laws of God and you can decide the most difficult ones only.*

Sometimes as parents we try to do too much. We need to learn to use the abilities of the household of God to help raise children. Moses was the father figure and a great man. But what he did was not good. You teach a child what the *way* is. Teach him who he is. Turn children loose but observe them. Keep them on leash but allow their hearts to lead them. Trust the heart that you have built in your children to lead them through the wildernesses. The heart is God's harness to keep children in contact with God and parents.

Moses' task, which was to teach all the children of Israel God's laws and ordinances, would have never been accomplished had not Moses shared the burden of education with other members of the household or church of God. Very few parents have raised any children alone. When using the Gospel Model, be on the lookout for churches, schools, teachers, clubs, and activities that will reinforce what you have taught children. Do not be afraid to shop around.

To look for the best for children is a good thing, but the best may not be obtainable when it comes to creating all surroundings for children. Moses' mother may have thought it was a terrible thing for her son to be raised and educated by Egyptians. With the heart of a Hebrew, Moses made good use of the things he learned from the Egyptians. Not all parents can afford to send children to private Christian schools, but any parent can send children to public schools with a heart that naturally seeks out the good and avoids the corrupt.

The question: what is God's *way* or manner of raising a child? The answer is found in biblical examples of godly parents who had an active faith as they instilled the qualities of *the way* into personality development of children. These parents taught that children could change their world and that they could obtain their goals in life.

God intended for parents and churches to participate to determine the personality of children. Children were not created to develop on their own. Parents and churches have everything to add to this process at the correct time. This is the reason that God made it natural for the strongest influence on children to be parents first and then fathers in the Lord secondly.

In the Bible, the household of David is one of the better examples of a family of maladaptive and adaptive personalities. A maladaptive personality is targeted for failure whereas an adaptive personality is marked for success. Here we identify David as a person able to adapt to many difficult situations— lions, bears, or giants. People might know who Jessie is in the Bible, that he was the father of David. Can you name any of his eight sons other than David? David was the only son who was well known because of his actions and his ability to adapt to difficult life situations. He was the one who had a heart to God's liking. And he was the one others depended on when there was no one left to kill giants. It was for both the good of the congregation of Israel and David that the children of Israel did not stop David from opposing the giant.

CHAPTER EIGHT

The Goals and Blessings of a Pure Heart

But Mary kept all these things, and pondered them in her heart.
(Luke 2:19)

And he went down with them, and came to Nazareth, and was subject unto them: but his mother kept all these sayings in her heart.
(Luke 2:5)

Preparation of the Heart

Jesus viewed the heart as a very active place, being continually the source of either good or evil. But the heart was not the source of both good and evil. When the mind attempted to mix good with evil or light with darkness, the entire heart becomes dark and evil.

But if thine eye be evil, thy whole body shall be full of darkness. If therefore the light that is in thee be darkness, how great is that darkness! (Matthew 6:23)

Paul referred to this confused state of the heart as a carnal mind that walked after the flesh leading only to destruction.

We do not want a confused-hearted child to follow the heart for, as James stated, a double-minded person is unstable in his ways (James 1:8). Children can allow their hearts to be their guide, providing they are functioning within the parameters of a pure heart. When Jesus inspected the fig tree and found no fruit, the tree withered away. Jesus knew that a tree that had no fruit had very weak and shallow roots and prophesied its future. Jesus knew there was something wrong with the fig tree but its lack of fruit told what type of tree it was. A heart that is not in harmony with God may appear to be saintly, but without the fruit, it is only an appearance (Matthew 21:19).

> And when he saw a fig tree in the way, he came to it, and found nothing thereon, but leaves only, and said unto it, Let no fruit grow on thee henceforward for ever. And presently the fig tree withered away. (Matthew 21:19)

Children who do not have the Gospel Model in their hearts will not bear proper fruit. Parents who do not have their hearts filled with good things have no chance of being fruitful parents. To be like a fig tree that is sick and withered is a result of being less than a person appears to be. The fig tree looked good but the substance within the tree was not capable of bearing fruit. To have confidence in child raising ability, parents simply need to have a pure heart. God promises to remove the old heart and to give you and your children a new heart, but you must walk and function within the structure of the Gospel Model.

Take note of how God placed good things in the heart of Mary. Mary was given the job of raising the Christ child. To insure Christ's future, Mary needed only to keep a vision of the *way* which the men of God and angels had told her. If parents do not see the future for their children, children may never learn to walk in the path of the gospel.

To prepare their hearts for service God gave great parents a vision for their children. Parents who do not know what to expect have not received a clear vision of the GOALS of parenting. The idea being, parents are to adopt a goal, purpose, or vision to be reached by parenting towards the fulfillment of the vision. The Gospel Model will make the vision clear. It is not only part of the message—the blessing itself—but it is a tool to deliver the message.

In the Bible parents told the babies vital to God's plans exactly what the purposes of God were. This guidance came from the hearts of parents stocked with visions of greatness. This knowledge, which was first stored in the hearts of parents, was enough to overcome all conditions in which these babies had to grow and mature. Babies cannot choose where they are born, but parents can direct lives by what they teach them. Moses' mother did not teach him how to rule Egypt. The king of Egypt did this. Moses' mother taught her son how to worship the one true God.

When it came time to choose between the crown of Egypt and freedom for the Hebrews, he knew which to choose. Moses knew that he was of the household of the people of God. Nothing his Egyptian parents could do would change this. Once Moses' personality was built within the household of God, he had God's blessing. He was safe. Moses was fashioned to obey God. When God called to Moses from the burning bush, Moses responded. In this respect all your children can be like Moses!

John the Baptist made the way for the Son of God, and Jesus completed the task for which He came into the world. Their parents explained God's plan to them. Explaining God's plan to children works. Giving children an explanation of why they exist provides them armor with which to ward off faulty leadership.

The Real Blessing

Knowledge of this *purpose*—the knowledge of how to raise children—was called the blessing, and began with Adam and Eve. The blessing then was passed down through the household of God's people. *The way* was God blessing the act of child rearing. This is the meaning of the blessing to Adam, Noah, and Abraham. In Genesis 18:18–19, *the way* continued as the children of Abraham are blessed as the angel of the Lord said:

> *Seeing that Abraham shall surely become a great and mighty nation, and all the nations of the earth shall be blessed in him? For I know him, that he will command his children and his household after him, and they shall keep the way of the LORD, to do justice and judgment; that the LORD may bring upon Abraham that which he hath spoken of him.*

This blessing to Abraham was a reinstatement of the blessing to Adam and Eve and also Noah. It was never intended for any parent to fail at child rearing, for God originally blessed Adam and Eve, which meant that God made Adam and Eve the prototype of perfect parents to bring children to the tree of eternal life. That is the true meaning of the following verse.

> And God blessed them, and God said unto them, Be fruitful, and multiply, and replenish the earth . . . (Genesis 1:28)

Child rearing was the blessing. The blessing was also the main and number one task of Noah. From the time of the flood, the history of mankind rested with Noah and his sons being fruitful and outstanding parents. Noah had the responsibility of bringing life back to the earth. Noah found *the way* since God made the same promise to him and his sons as God did to Adam and Eve.

And God blessed Noah and his sons, and said unto them, Be fruit-ful, and multiply, and replenish the earth. (Genesis 9:1)

Later, this was the same blessing mentioned in the Bible when God first blessed Abraham, when his name was still Abram in Genesis 12:1–3. Here God made it plain to Abram that he was no longer to follow the way of his family, but to walk before God in a different *way*.

And I will make of thee a great nation, and I will bless thee, and make thy name great; and thou shalt be a blessing: . . . and in thee shall all families of the earth be blessed.

This blessing of Abraham was for you, for families, and nations. That means it was for schools, jobs, churches, and civic clubs. God emphasized the universal use of this pattern by including Abraham's descendents in the blessing. The blessing so often talked about in the Bible was the ability to raise children. As parents raise children today to have an active faith, they are passing the blessing of correct child rearing on to their children and nations. They are creating the household of God. They are being assertive.

The *way* to raise children is natural because it is blessed. But the whole process is not self-perpetuating. It must be passed on. Listen to what God said about Abraham and the *way* of the blessing (Genesis 18:19).

For I know him, that he will command his children and his household after him, and they shall keep the way of the LORD, to do justice and judgment; that the LORD may bring upon Abraham that which he hath spoken of him.

Why did God have Moses drill into the minds and hearts of the children of Israel the laws of God? Was it because God knew that children could and often do turn quickly out of *the way*? Is there a specific thing God wants us to drill into the minds of our children? God intervened to bring His children back into the *way* many times. Prevention turned out to be one of God's best methods of intervention. He installed prevention into their minds by providing trials and challenges to strengthen His children's resolve to stay focused on reaching their goal of going to the Promised Land.

Never doubt it for a minute, there is a battle going on all the time for control of the minds and hearts of children. The demons of society are actively pulling children to destruction. Drugs, tobacco, alcohol, pornography, and violence on TV and in movies are all threats to children. You do not have to believe in God to know that these evil demons are after your children. Jesus called these evil things sin and the works of the devil. Social workers see these as symptoms of a sick society or a dysfunctional family. That is why Jesus wants every parent to build a perfect house or perfect structure in children's minds so children can resist being taken over by the negative influences in life. For this reason alone, children need to have the blessing passed on to them by parents using the Gospel Model

Samuel was told as a baby that he would be a light to the house of God and a blessing to the nation of Israel. When it came time to leave his mother's side, he did not rebel but lived to anoint the future kings of Israel. Early in life David understood God's ways, as his parents taught him to care for sheep. By slaying the lion and bear that came after his sheep, David learned how to trust the Lord and protect a nation from giants. Boldness to trust in the Lord can be learned by children. All the great babies in the Bible had to overcome obstacles before they came of age to do their great deeds. The secret for children is to be given a simple but active faith, found in the Gospel Model, which allows them to kill a few lions and bears.

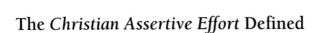

CHAPTER NINE

Christian Assertive Effort

The *Christian Assertive Effort* Defined

The *Christian Assertive Effort* is the attempt Christians make in planting the Gospel Model into the hearts of all segments of society as well as the hearts of parents and children. A *Christian Assertive Effort* is the vehicle for the Gospel Model. The good news is that Christ belongs in hearts.

The only way to get the message of Jesus Christ to the heart of society is to take it there. Without the maximum *effort*, the Gospel Model will fall in unfertile and untilled ground. Christians must do things to prepare the ground for sowing. The Gospel Model promises to heal children of mental and emotional illness, to train children in a way that makes them successful in what they do, to immunize them from the bad effects of everyday experiences, and to build them up like a strong house built on a firm foundation. If society is friendly to them by being more Christian than otherwise, the seed in the hearts of children will do well. The Gospel Model in society will make children kind, not spiteful; generous, not stingy; hopeful, not sad. But, Christians must prepare society to receive children. You can help get this done in your community. The *Christians Assertive Effort* involves getting the message through to society as a starting point. God approved of the maximum effort. Why else would God send his Son? This is proof that God cares.

> *For God so loved the world, that he gave his only begotten Son, that whosoever believeth in him should not perish, but have everlasting life.* (John 3:16)

God sent his Son into the world as the ultimate effort. God planted His Son in society first. Common sense tells us to prepare the ground for seeds to a great harvest. The same analogy applies to raising children the Bible way. Parents can best sow seed in children if at the same time they sow seeds in society. Christ came into society to save all men. Just like God sent John the Baptist and the prophets to prepare society for Christ, God now wants to send the *Christian Assertive Effort*.

Some people by nature are skeptical of do-gooders; their first response to the *Christian Assertive Effort* will not necessarily be supportive. Some have a personality that is built to be in opposition to things. Opposition is the most common response for SINS, which is the type of person Satan tries to recruit to destroy the hope of Christians.

Opposition to God's plan is subtle. A neighbor's son developed cancer. The neighbor had recently turned down an opportunity to give to the local cancer fund. It was annoying that someone would come to his door asking for money. The man demonstrated his opposition to those making the effort to fight cancer. He did not want to be bothered. Do you think the neighbor might have feelings of regret and guilt? How will he feel in asking the cancer fund for assistance? He did ask and became the number one supporter of the cancer fund.

In the *Christian Assertive Effort* you will find a way to save children from at-risk factors, to immunize them against the effects of bad life events, to build self-confidence and self-esteem, and to train citizens to be a blessing to the nation.

Make it your purpose to assert the model of Christ in society. The Gospel Model never stops working. There is no model without action. A verb is always associated with God. He is the great I AM. The model of God says you are what you do. You are only an assertive Christian if you *do* sowing. Teachers in public and private schools can work this model into their curriculum and lesson plans where it will have a tremendous therapeutic impact. Embrace this model for your community. You will be adopting a way of life that will not fail you in raising children, living in the work place, and in building a strong home, school and church. Embracing this model is the *Christian Assertive Effort*.

Sowing Seed in Society

The parable recorded in Matthew's Gospel, chapter 13, is what sowing seed in society is like. The field is society, not a geographical position. Some of the seed sown will not bear fruit. The *Christian Assertive Effort* will be attacked by society. Many will reject the *Christian Assertive Effort* outright making reference to all the seed that did not produce or spring forth. "Everything we have tried did not work," they say. "How is this going to work?"

Surely they are not talking about the image of Christ, the Gospel Model. Everything Christ does will work. Jesus said to keep planting. The seeds of harvest will be of a hundred, sixty, and thirty fold. In light of a few failures, be assertive. The overall harvest will pay off all the debits of farming. Jesus wants us to be assertive and sow.

Parents can direct the seed to fertile ground and provide it the best chance to spring forth. Seed can be placed where thorns will not likely spring up and destroy young seed. Can you see what Jesus was saying in the parable of the seed? Public schools do not have to choke off the word of God. Politics can be a tool that belongs to Christian households. Just keep placing seed where it will do the most good. Christ the Gospel Model will show you how!

Even though you teach children about God and His goodness, Satan is looking for a crack in the ground to sow his seed and lifestyle. How did a great man of God such as David give birth to such a dysfunctional family? The fact that he did still shocks us today. David should have seen this coming because he knew he would reap as he had sown. David fornicated with another man's wife, killed her husband to hide his sin, and in doing so, lost not only the child of his fornication, but most of his family to the scourge of bad seed that grew into SINS rather than GOALS. David's son raped his sister, whose brother killed the rapist, who himself was eventually killed in attempting to steal the Jewish empire away from his father. David caused or planted all this confusion and grief by planting seed incorrectly when he adopted a SINS way of living. Although he was in the clutches of SINS for a short time, he did a lifetime of damage to his family.

Consider the parents of John Walker. In an interview on CNN the parents of American terrorist John Walker admitted that they raised their child to think freely, to choose the religion of his choice, and to make his own moral decisions. This is an anti-Christ response. He was free to choose to fight against his country, to join the Talliban and Al Qaeda forces that brought down the World Trade Center buildings. If John Walker's parents could choose now for their son a fundamentalist Christian point of view rather than the free-thinking process of SINS, the choice would be easier to make. The choices children will make ultimately depend on the choices parents have already made. Do you see how the Walkers set their son up to fail? Do not make their mistake. Be in control of your children.

Parents are to be in control of the family just like Adam and Eve were created to be in control of the first family. The commands to *multiply* and *subdue* mean parents are to be in control of children (Genesis 1:28). How could parents be responsible to God for Proverbs 22:6, if they were not meant to be in control? That is what *subdue* means. The commandment to be parents is stated, [You] *Train up a child in the way he should go: and when he is old, he will not depart from it.*

If children are just allowed to grow up, given freedom to become whatever they want to be, we are neglecting the plan of God for rearing children. Parents must give of their spirit and knowledge to children as they grow and mature. Children were meant to be part of a family that is controlled by adults. The structured foundation of the family provides direction for its members and control for parents.

The Bible teaches that if parents do not take charge of their children's lives, other forces will. The life of John Walker is an excellent illustration of parents not in control. Survey the most successful families in the Bible. It is clear that parents were always in control. The moral understandings of a family do not come from children but from parents. Whenever children are permitted to be in control, the outcomes are generally disastrous.

Look once more at King David's family. Tamara was the daughter raped by her brother Amnon, who was later killed by his brother Absalom, who later attempted to take the kingdom of Israel away from his father King David. This short epic of children being out of control ends with the sad epitaph of King David crying for the death of his son Absalom, who had to die to prevent the overthrow of the kingdom. Do you see any similarities between David and the Walkers? Do you now understand what the lack of control means?

> *And the king was much moved, and went up to the chamber over the gate, and wept: and as he went, thus he said, O my son Absalom, my son, my son Absalom! would God I had died for thee, O Absalom, my son, my son!* (2 Samuel 18:33)

The Walkers would probably die for their son as David would have for Absalom. Children need parents to live for them, not die; to live a life as an example for them, to be a part of their lives, to train and direct them. That is how parents gain control. Parents must be the center and matrix of power in the family. Children cannot be allowed to be in control and go their own ways; they must derive guidelines from the center of the family. Effective parents do not promote situations which allows children to self-destruct and move towards utter chaos. Parents who acquiesce to every whim of children are forcing them to make decisions they are not prepared to make. These children will pursue selfish and worldly goals. Remember that control is GOALS.

CHAPTER TEN

Obstacles: What Did You Expect?

Paul said Jesus Christ was the model or *form of God* (Philippians 4:6). Form, pattern, model, structure, these are one and the same. That Paul points this out is no surprise for he was the apostle who talked about the Old Covenant being a schoolmaster to bring us to the knowledge of Christ. Paul confirmed that Christ showed Himself as a pattern for them who were to believe in Him. For believing in this holy pattern, Christians were to receive everlasting life (1 Timothy 1:16). In Titus 2:7 the Bible says for Christians to show themselves as patterns of good works. In Hebrews 8:5, these words spoken to Moses are significant: *See, saith he, that thou make all things according to the pattern shewed to thee in the mount.*

Obstacles occur to stop you. Obstacles are meant for evil but God uses them for good. Instead of stumbling blocks, God makes them steppingstones. When SINS stops us, it hurts God. The war is between God and the devil. We know who is going to win. Stand still! Ignore obstacles and keep planting seed, and opposition to your efforts will perish with the demise of SINS in society.

Opposition from a Lack of Knowledge

Sunday at church, while people were filing out to go home, Connie, an expecting mother for the first time, expressed to me her desire to raise her child the way the Lord wanted her baby to be raised. "I want to raise my child the way God wants him raised," she said while showing a great deal of anxiety and apprehensiveness. She really needed to know about the Gospel Model. Satan convinced everybody around Connie that no one knew how God wanted her child to be raised. The people in her life knew the Bible very well and knew how to raise children, but on the other hand they did not know they knew. Martin Luther knew about faith, being a scholar of the Bible but he received an awakening of how to make use of faith. Has Satan convinced you that it is not possible for you to be a guide to parents in raising children? Connie deserved an answer from God's Word. What then should be the role of pastors and elders in the church?

The outstanding example of successful children in the Bible begins with God preparing their parents for parenthood before their children arrive. His mother Hannah dedicated Samuel to God before his birth (1 Samuel 1). John the Baptist's purpose was told to his parents before John was conceived. The chosen Mary was instructed by God to bring the Christ child into the world, how to raise Him and what His name should be. Not only did Mary have the information from angels but the awesome impact of the prophets who foretold of Christ's appearing contributed to how she must raise Jesus (Luke 1).

Similar to the aforementioned babies, most Christians believe there are no accidental births and that God has a special plan for every baby. Christian parents who act on biblical principles of faith to instruct their children towards God's plan for their lives are choosing for their children the good rather than the evil that is in the world. Ministers, Christian teachers, and parents must dig this information out of the Bible and organize it to make it plain to the caretakers of children. This knowledge is not private. It belongs to all of God's children. As soon as Connie began to make plans for her child by selecting goals for the child, her job of raising children became much easier. Her plans were not to make the child the president of the U.S.A. but to plan the planting of seeds so the child would have the personality of GOALS.

The best way for a pastor to serve Connie was to give her good reasons to learn the Gospel Model. If she could see the many positive things the model prepared her to do for her child, it would be enough to motivate her to accept and learn the model.

The actual problems of the Quick Success children were easily solved. The difficult obstacle was getting parents to look at children from a new point of few. Parents had tried everything imaginable with children. Experts were plentiful and available, but it took the Gospel Model and the willingness to use it to make the solutions simple. Nothing the parents did was revolutionary or new. When they used the light from the Gospel Model, quick results followed. It was the type of knowledge that never fails.

More Confusion

Connie was an intelligent girl, a schoolteacher, and familiar with the academic principles of human growth and development. She had studied the many branches of psychology. She had been trained in methods and techniques of motivation and learning and how to identify children who were academically at risk. Yet, her anxieties demonstrated that she lacked the confidence or know-how to raise her own child. With the knowledge she had, she sensed something else was needed. Her church and pastor could find this for her.

Connie knew how professional psychologists and authorities on the subject of child rearing were required scientifically to support their opinions. She knew professionals offer advice on raising children only after years of studying, testing, experimenting, validating surveys, and scrutinizing the scientific research of others. With the vast knowledge available to her, raising children looked like a more omnibus job than it was. With the Gospel Model Connie was about to learn a method of pulling all this knowledge together and learn to use it with confidence.

Knowing about child rearing did not mean that Connie could successfully do it. There were many portions of false knowledge in the world to cast disparaging influences on her efforts. She was familiar with a number of religious leaders who posed as authorities on every issue under the sun. Often, religious leaders have the opinion that the status of their position qualifies them as advisors on all subjects. The news media is always full of stories of religious cult leaders who have been responsible for bringing disastrous occurrences into the lives of their followers. Society is full of so-called experts who turn out to be cult leaders rather than social scientists or ministers. To avoid this, Connie had to become the expert.

If Connie was apprehensive, whose advice could she trust? Preachers' children have the same statistics of success as other children and appear to have no greater advantage over other children. If there is great truth about child rearing in the Bible, should not the men of God do better than the average parent at child rearing? This speaks to the fact that the purveyors of the Word have not gleaned the model of God well enough from the Scriptures to assert the special advantage of child rearing found in the Bible. Could Connie be safe in following her pastor's advice on the topic of child rearing? Connie only needed a structured method to free her to use her own knowledge.

We are back to the real question Connie was asking. How can young parents safely find information and advice about rearing children? Both the scientific and theological arenas are filled with discarded theories that have been found to be unreliable after having led many down an incorrect path. Connie was looking for a strategy that would tell her what to do if something went wrong in the growth and development of her child. She wanted assurance that she could prevent learning delays, bad behavior, and emotional disorders. She wanted an effective defense against the multiple at-risk factors that would threaten the growth and maturity of her child. Connie was looking beyond childhood and into the adult life. She was searching for the Gospel Model amidst massive misinformation and confusion, which acted as a great obstacle.

There had to be a *way* and Connie found it in GOALS. GOALS, as you remember, is symbolic for *God's Oriented Assertive Life Style* and is synonymous with adaptive explanatory lifestyles that fight off learned helplessness. When the pastor made the Gospel Model a part of his church's common knowledge, she quickly chose her method of raising children.

The church and God's people have the answers to the questions that parents are asking. We need to act like we have the knowledge so people will believe us. In using the Gospel Model, you are what you do. By assuming the expert role about raising children, SINS is being rejected for children. Many circumstances and situations prevent the Christian message from getting through to parents. The lack of confidence should not be one of the obstacles. You may not be the expert but the model you are following is, if it is the Gospel Model.

Can parents trust and have confidence in Bible knowledge for guidance? If salvation depends on the trustworthiness of the Bible, then the Bible can be trusted as information for how to raise children. In fact, parents and caretakers of children are taking the smallest risk of all by following the Gospel Model in raising children.

Societal Obstacles

The parents of our children of Quick Success I, II, and III were a cross section of economic and educational status. Some had post-college education and others did not. What common characteristic these parents had was that their children were in trouble. Soon after we had one success with the Gospel Model, another parent would come looking for the same type of help. There was a new understanding in our school that was appealing to the needy, regardless of social status.

Poverty, social status, educational levels, and ethnic and cultural differences act as hindrances only if God's people allow it. Seekers of this message have no race, creed, or social status. At-risk children come from all levels of society. When a house with children inside is burning a fireman is never asked if he has a Ph.D. or if he has a million dollars in the bank nor does the fireman ask what the social status of children is. The church must overcome, through infiltration and an assertive effort, to begin pulling children out of a burning fire. How thoroughly the church prepares and informs itself will determine how clearly the message of Jesus Christ gets through or infiltrates to the target area, which is the hearts of children and of society. God is waiting for the church to be armed with a clear understanding of the Gospel Model and to make the correct assertion of the Word into society. God wants us to infiltrate the world with the Gospel Model.

There are many circumstances under which children must be raised, but there is only one model or pattern that God wants us to use on all children. Circumstances sometimes force parents to raise children a certain way. Parents of wealth provide opportunities for children which parents with low incomes could never dream of providing. Children raised in the lowest segments of society will always wonder what the lives of the privileged child is like. This is a fact of life.

Make no mistake about it. The failure of a child is the most painful event that parents experience whether they have wealth or not. Whether rich or poor, with an active faith and appropriate goals, parents can avoid failure as a way of life in children regardless of economic and social status. Parents can raise children to be protected from failure even when they cannot make them wealthy. The best chance for success is to give children the *proper instruction* from God.

Many children will be forced to look at the way they have been raised as an obstacle that must be overcome. Create for children the ability to rise from the situation in which they are raised by teaching the model of God. They do not have to view life as if fate has dealt them a bad hand. Failure, poor, weak, and scared are all situations learned by the minds of children. The family tradition of being on welfare from generation to generation is an example of children having learned a situation of despair. Children who break from the welfare roles are examples of children becoming over-comers. Those who escaped learned something unique about their existence and used this uniqueness to motivate them to success.

That unique thing that tells children to be successful and climb the ladder to success distinguishes and separates children who were taught correctly about God. We are mainly talking about personality building rather than economics, social status, or college degrees. What type of personality will children have?

It is not a matter of wealth or privilege that a child has that gives him an advantage. CNN reported on Monday, September 10, 2001 that sixty to seventy percent of children who were victims of street violence, abuse, and sexual crimes were members of the middle or upper classes. Traditionally, such failures were associated with low social and economic status.

Children from wealthy families regularly fail in life or are made victims. Perhaps the use of drugs has contributed to this. Parents can send their children to the best schools and colleges and they still do not succeed, while at the same time others are learning to scratch and claw their way out of poverty and towards the top of the ladder of success. Whether rich or poor there is *a way* that can be instilled in a child that keeps him on *the way* to success and protects him against failure. That is what God wants Christian parents to provide for children. That is what the Bible means when it commands us to train a child. A Gospel Model child is the advantaged child.

Obstacles of Trends and Fads

Connie with the Gospel Model learned to bring Scripture and science together so as to be able to discriminate what is good for her child. Both harmful fads and good science tend to come with every new generation. How to distinguish between the two is not so simple. Frontier folk seemed to approve of the out-to-the-woodshed method of discipline and training children, while modern discipline methods are a more *time out* approach. You will find adults who have endured both these philosophies as children. A rigid, stern type of discipline has received both praise and condemnation; the same can be said of the more tolerant and permissive approach. All in all, it can be said that both approaches have met with success and failure. Only the Gospel Model has had no failures.

Our great nation has originated from both points of view which suggest that the disagreement over the way children should be disciplined might not be relevant to whether or not success will follow them into adulthood. There are more significant and stabilizing forces involved in child rearing which only the Gospel Model can identify for parents. The stabilizing components of the Gospel Model create success in both philosophies of discipline.

A good example of this situation is addressed in Quick Success II where Matthew's family was trapped between two opposing philosophies of rearing children. The solution for Matthew came when his parents chose a direction of child rearing different from that of either parent. The principal inserted the Gospel Model into their formula of planning. The component the parents inserted was from the Gospel Model. Matthew learned who he was and why he must behave as asked. Goals were established and Matthew enjoyed the praise of his scout master, teachers, and parents.

Fads come and go. The incidence of mistakes by professionals advising parents on how to raise children is as long as history itself. When religion has been blindly mixed with public education, the historical results have not been very rewarding. All one has to do is survey the literature of the Puritan community of early American history to know of the guilt complexes, the shattering of self-esteem, and psychological fears that an over-zealous religious education placed into the minds of children. Nathaniel Hawthorne is excellent reading on this point of view.

In spite of a history of trial and error, acceptance and rejection, there is a large core of information that has survived on which parents can safely rely. There are also a host of bad child rearing methods and theories that have survived. The problem of identifying either the bad fads or good scientific methods remains a problem unless one uses an appropriate model as a guide. In the Gospel Model, the parent asks whether or not the ascribed method supports GOALS.

The Gospel Model is scientifically sound and a true scientific model is also biblically sound. As a general rule any method or model that meets both scientific requirements and Gospel Model goals will be a reliable approach. With such a model, parents can safely strengthen their children against the influences of failure!

An important fact is that parents can know what affects child-rearing methods are having on children when using God's model. In God's model there are no blind spots.

The Gospel Model is the same model Mary used with Jesus, Abraham with Isaac, and the mother of Moses with her son. Parents can actually immunize children against learning helplessness, which creates slow learning children, low self-esteem, and the urge to give up easily! This model gives parents the ability to abolish many obstacles before they originate. A model of raising children, which is preventive in nature, is far superior to methods of intervention. Parents can, however, know when and how to helpfully intervene within the emotional growth of children, that is, if all this great information is presented to parents in a useable way. The Bible teaches that the church is best suited to use the Gospel Model.

Obstacles to Utilization

Utilization is the key. Satan does not mind that you know the Gospel Model, as long as it is not used. Satan hates the *Assertive Christian Effort* for this reason. The Gospel Model provides for parents a well-explained blueprint or map to follow, but it must be followed. There is power in the Gospel Model as evidenced by the ease with which our parents of Quick Success had quick results. All three sets of parents were able to intervene to stop the development of more serious personality problems of their children. William's mother knew where to go to check the wisdom of the new methods. Did William have a spoiled-brat syndrome? William's therapist thought so. The strategy she used was not earthshaking, but it was simply aimed directly at the problem.

Matthew had learned to act as if he was depressed, having a learned depressed personality. His mother read a book called *Parent Power.* What she knew about the Gospel Model taught her that *Parent Power* could provide a safe strategy to extinguish the learned personality syndrome of her son. Although the scout leader and teacher may have thought they were major factors in Matthew's recovery, it was his mother following the Gospel Model that did the trick.

Ryan's mother discovered that her child was really wonderful and not at all in need of something called a transition class. His problems were so obvious yet several teachers, two school administrators, and a guidance councilor failed to see Ryan's problem. Ryan's principal of one day, using the Gospel Model to view Ryan's behavior, knew exactly what was needed.

What guided all three parents through a maze of information was the Gospel Model. As caretakers of children, to assert this model, you need only to become more familiar with all functional parts of the model. More successes with children should be anticipated.

Just like any road map, a person can get lost if the symbols on the map are a mystery to the reader of the map. Those who handle the Word of God should be the very best at utilization of the model and at getting this message through to the church community in the same way Pastor John Doe did in chapter one and two. The explanation of the Gospel Model needs to be commonplace. Sunday school teachers, babysitters, and neighbors should talk the language of the Gospel Model daily. It should be at least as commonly known as John 3:16.

The more information parents have about child rearing and the various parts of the Gospel Model, the more of an expert they become. Allegiance will be paid to the giver of parental knowledge that works well with both normal children and children at risk. That is why the church of Jesus Christ needs to be the one to gather information and pass it on to parents so it can be utilized.

The church can bridge many gaps that exist between God's understandings about children and the professional's point of view. James taught his church to take care of at-risk children as a prerequisite for purity (James 1:27). With the Gospel Model, the church can make religion and secular jargon meaningful and useful. All the parents in Quick Success I, II, and III understood the professional effort that was being made by the principal, but only after the Gospel Model was explained to them did they have success with raising children. Only then could they utilize the information they already knew.

The gaps in reading and comprehension levels of parents can be overcome by using models. On radio, TV, in newspapers, we keep hearing that the average American reads on a seventh or eighth grade level. Producers of movies prepare their scripts to match this level of sophistication, which enables the average American to understand what is happening during a TV show or movie. The expert in childhood psychology does not have the luxury of adjusting the script to meet the intellectual level of parents. The professional psychologist must use the scientific terms of his discipline and adhere to the limitations that science places upon him while explaining the psychological principles of child rearing. In most cases this level of speaking or writing is far above the intellectual level of the average American. The church needs to be prepared to bridge this intellectual gap so the message of God will get through. Just as radio and TV have bridged the gap by using a vocabulary suitable for the audience, the Gospel Model can do this for the church. Every Christian should be able to use the Gospel Model.

The scientific studies from which the professional expert derives his opinion must meet the scrutiny of the scientific method. If you have any doubts about how complicatedly written these scientific studies are, simply go to the local library. Read through any scientific journal, and you will see why scholars, who possess graduate degrees, must carefully, painstakingly, and repeatedly read and re-read the articles in these journals in order to understand the information given. The prerequisite for college students to enroll in a fundamental course in child development is usually another course called general psychology. Most Americans do not read on a college level, have not had the prerequisite course, and do not understand the technical vocabulary of a course called human growth and development.

The confusion in America's culture tells us that many experts in psychology have failed to grasp well enough this information to be able to pass it on to parents. Can we really expect the average American to understand the information which teachers, psychologists, and the church is providing to parents concerning child rearing unless we begin talking in understandable terms? It will take more than what the secular world has to offer. It will take the assistance of the Gospel Model to deliver the message.

Obstacles to Intervention

A basic problem for many parents who have the will and courage to intervene in the educational and emotional growth of children is that they do not know where to start. In the public schools it is often taboo for teachers to involve themselves with parents of emotionally needy children. Teachers too often have become harmfully involved with children because they lack an adequate means to evaluate children emotionally. Teachers too often see emotional needs to be reserved for the counselor who is usually an educational counselor and not a therapist at all.

Without the guiding light of the Gospel Model, many serious events are viewed as minor events. For example, O. M. Terry beat me up on the steps of the first grade room. The reason he beat me up was that no one had explained to me that I could not always be first in line to go into the classroom when the recess bell rang. At home I was the baby and always was first. The fight was not really big in the eyes of the teacher who handled this as a minor event. However, the residual effect on me was that I learned that the first grade was not a good place for me.

Other minor events occurred and I learned that school was a bad place for children and that teachers were not people on whom you should depend for safety. I would have learned to fight back but the teacher said to fight would result in a spanking.

From this one minor event began the learning of a very global belief that getting an education was going to be difficult. The teacher did stop the fight, but my fears and serious concerns were overlooked. If there had been a teacher trained in the Gospel Model, I have no doubt that my life would have been better and much different. Any word of encouragement would have made a difference. There was no way for me to think about learning to read, for my fears of school dominated my mind. Learning to read for me came in high school.

As a teacher I was very sensitive to the needs of at-risk children. Many opportunities to intervene in their lives passed by me because there was not available to me a means to view the long-lasting effects of events that were taking place in my classroom. Sometimes a simple word of encouragement or explanation is all that is needed to turn the life of children toward a different direction. Adults are generally willing to intervene but do not understand the significance of what is taking place.

Here is how our school stumbled into intervening with children who were prone to fight. As long as they were fighting, they were not learning to solve conflicts. At the school there was a historical and sacred rule that if two children were involved in a fight, the one deemed to be the aggressor was given a paddling. This did not stop fights, but did create arguments over who actually started the fight. If it could not be determined who started the fight, which was the case most of the time, both students were paddled. This did not stop fighting. Finally it was my decision that in a fight that neither party would be paddled. If either student were to be paddled, parents would have to come from home to do the paddling. Things were going to change.

A very strange thing occurred. Children who were notorious for fighting began to behave differently. Groups of children who usually fought to settle their problems were now coming to the principal's office to discuss who was right or wrong over serious issues. Previously, the children knew that fighting was going to get somebody a spanking. Previously children knew that a spanking was coming and they were more interested in avoiding a spanking than they were in settling their differences. With the threat of a spanking removed, children were free to face the problems and to settle the differences by focusing on the real issues. Do you think the new behavior of the principal had a righteous affect on the children?

The actual conflicts children have are really good for them, theoretically speaking, if adults have been wise enough to allow an avenue in which children can solve the conflict or tolerate the outcome of conflict. With the Gospel Model it could be seen to add a spanking to conflicts of children was detracting from their natural goal of finding a solution. Our children wanted the approval of parents and adults and sought to demonstrate that they were mature enough to solve their own problems.

This is not an argument against spanking children. But you will recall that Ryan of Quick Success was spanked fifteen times by the principal before Christmas. With all the other events Ryan had to deal with, the threat of a spanking surely made conflicts between him and adults unsolvable. When all extraneous stresses were removed, Ryan became what his mother called a perfect child. With practice, using the Gospel Model, child rearing becomes very rewarding.

In a rural school of about five hundred students, it is difficult to imagine how much the public talked about the no spanking policy. The no spanking policy worked. Parents began to talk about something new the principal was using for discipline other than spanking. An opportunity for giving a Christian testimony was created each time a parent or student asked a question about the new discipline policy.

Christians need to talk it up. Some needy person may overhear and desire to know more about this model. I have learned that people are listening when conversation is about helping children. No matter how negative parents felt toward school authority, they were always willing to listen to anybody who could help them understand and correct the developmental flaws in their children. By talking it up, it is possible that you are sowing seeds of intervention for other parents.

Religion is a matter of faith. People believe what the Bible tells them as a matter of faith. To believe Proverbs 22:6: *Train up a child in the way he should go: and when he is old, he will not depart from it,* does not require the scientific certainty that the study of psychology requires. How to use this information, how to glean it from the Scriptures, does require a good deal of common sense; somebody has to study the problem for the solution to be made clear. This is the role of pastors and teachers.

*And he gave some, apostles; and some, prophets; and some, evangelists; and some, **pastors and teachers**; For the perfecting of the saints, for the work of the ministry, for the edifying of the body of Christ.*
(Ephesians 4:11–12, emphasis added)

Pseudo Science is an Obstacle

We have already referred to the danger of cults and what they claim the Bible has to say about child rearing. Bogus science and pseudo religion are evil. It is common knowledge that certain parents have denied children medical treatment due to religious opinions gathered from the Bible. Some of these children have died as a result of poor wisdom in interpreting the Scripture. Actually, I think most common sense parents feel safer knowing the safest wisdom that is in the Bible is validated by scientific research. The Gospel Model must be communicated clearly to parents. The first thing that must be made clear is that the Gospel Model is good science. To live by faith does not mean that you live in disharmony with science.

God created science so man would have a way to explain the secrets of the universe God created. Adam needed a lot of knowledge in order to follow God's instructions properly. After receiving this knowledge, Adam simply needed to trust God that God's *way* would work. God put His approval on the scientific method in the Garden of Eden when God said to Adam:

> *Be fruitful, and multiply, and replenish the earth, and subdue it: and have dominion over the fish of the sea, and over the fowl of the air, and over every living thing that moveth upon the earth.* (Genesis 1:27)

There is no doubt that God expects man to be in control of God's creation. Having dominion over the earth was the knowledge contained in science and given to Adam. God laid down rules (science) for Adam to follow in subduing the earth and having dominion or control. When Adam did not follow the rules, he lost control of everything including his family and most importantly his children. It is sad how Cain grew up to hate his brother Able who loved God. When Cain slew Able and brought the first death into the world, this was a great tragedy. This could have been avoided had Adam followed the scientific formula that God provided.

In the epistle to the Romans 1:20, Paul points out that the things of God can be known by science. Early Christians did not have a

blind faith as some might suppose, but they used science to vali-
date the Word of God. Just like the Word of God, good science can
be trusted. It is clear from 1 Timothy 6:20 that the apostle Paul
considered beliefs that did not correspond to the Word of God or
science to be "science falsely so called" which was pseudo science.
Paul believed we should be always challenged to interpret the Bible
in balance with true science. This is the only safe way to avoid
being led out of *the way* by either faulty religious beliefs or faulty
science. Where science correctly speaks, it will not contradict the
Bible. When the Bible is correctly read, it will not oppose good
science. Parents and caretakers must explore both the Word of
God and science to discover God's safe way to raise children.

God has a definite plan in which He deals with his children.
Parents should have the same plan. Scientific studies in child
psychology have discovered the dynamic facts of God's plan.
Observation is the first step in the scientific method. Observation is first in God's plan too. Paul said we could see the invisible things of God from things that were (Romans 1:19). Psychology
is the science of human behavior; its research method is basically
the observation of behavior. This is what Paul meant when he said
that the visible things that occurred could allow us to see the invisible things of God. In other words, man could discover and deduce scientific laws. The basic laws of psychology were discovered
by science, but God created these laws.

> *For the invisible things of him from the creation of the world are*
> *clearly seen, being understood by the things that are made.* (Ro-
> mans 1:20)

Invisible laws, like the law of gravity, cannot be seen with
eyes; but these laws are as real as a tree, a house, towers, or
mountains. The invisible things of God are ideas in minds of
children. Invisible things can be taught and planted into the

minds of children. Knowledge of invisible things constitutes a special type of knowledge, which creates a unique style of living. Knowledge of the model that God wants parents to utilize in training children is a special knowledge which can be planted in the minds of children just as a tree can be planted in the ground.

If Christians talk it up about the Gospel Model it can be commonly known as the scientific method or the Constitution of the U.S.A. No obstacle in society can stop the message from getting through, providing Christians talk about the Gospel Model as if it were as common as the Constitution and the Bill of Rights. Most Americans know what their rights are from familiarity with national documents.

As remarkable as it may be, many citizens have never read the Constitution or the Bill of Rights. But they know what their freedoms are, and this, from the fact that people talk about the rights given to them by God and the Constitution of the United States. Getting the message through to Christian parents means the teachers of the gospel need to communicate the Gospel Model better. The subject needs to be talked about and made common.

CHAPTER ELEVEN

Christian Education—Is It Enough?

H ome schooling and Christian private schooling is a great thing but there can be a problem in that this type of schooling does not guarantee the production of a successful Christian student or parent. Too often the efforts Christians are making to educate children in a nurturing atmosphere is done by using a humanistic model that denies Christian principles. To teach absolute values, which are noted in the Constitution, with a model of behavior that denies the existence of any absolutes is a contradiction. That is what Christians who teach in the public schools are asked to do. What really makes a Christian education different is that children learn GOALS. It is entirely possible for Christian educators in Christian schools and public schools to miss the point.

Christian educators need to quickly gain an understanding of what they are really doing. The time is ready for Christians to be the salt of the earth. It is time for Christians to provide a suitable understanding of God's way of raising children. The Gospel Model of behavior is that *way*. Something is missing in many Christian schools and Christian home schooling. The missing link is GOALS. What is creeping in is SINS: *Satan's Inadequate Naturalistic Style* or

139

Schemes. Satan can assert his schemes and lifestyle while operating within the borders of a Christian school or home schooling. Christians are warned to watch out for Satan. He is subtle. Wherever the Word is being installed, Satan will be there to confuse people.

Christian characteristics being progressively placed into the personality makeup of children and adults is a Christian education. Satan is busy building a case in society to disallow the mentioning of God's value system in our schools. Satan does not want a clear view of God's ways to be known, which is why Satan blocks Christian education. The placing, asserting, and instilling of Jesus Christ into the hearts and minds of children is a Christian education.

Is Christian education enough? The answer is yes. However, a Christian education begins with parents. There is more educational emphasis placed on training parents in the Bible than there is for training children. The point being is that Christians need to find the parents of children like those of William, Matthew and Ryan of Quick Success and educate them. Pastor John Doe's church began first by telling parents the good news of how to raise children the Bible way.

Also, every school's curriculum, either private or public, can be turned into a Christian effort, if Christian teachers know how to use the model of Christ. Christians are to be subtle in much the same way as the devil is subtle when he imposes humanism on the public schools. Although the vast majority of society rejects humanism, Satan has made the world think it is required to follow its tenants. The belief of humanism is that man, not God, is the universal authority of human morality. Humanists do not openly say they reject God, but quietly expect the rejection of Christian values to be part of public education.

Christians need to be wise as snakes, harmless as doves, and secretive if need be, to the point of not letting society on the left know what society on the right is doing (Matthew 6 and 10). You can quietly urge children and parents to accept the Gospel Model into their hearts. The Roman Empire did not care what Jesus was teaching until it was too late for them to stop the spreading of the gospel. Go into the world and be wise! Teach society about God whether a few like it or not.

The Christian private schools should provide training for parents and teachers who labor in the public schools. The parents who have children going to public schools need the same training that is offered in the private Christian schools. The great thing about Christ is that He spreads His wings into the public domain through Christians teaching in public schools. Private Christian schools should also adopt the goal to influence public schools.

In some cases, many Christian schools function too similarly to public schools. The real difference in the two schools is not the number of times prayer and Bible reading take place. It is the philosophical basis upon which a school is built that makes it Christian. There is a book in the Bible where God is not mentioned one time, but it is a holy book and part of the Bible. The testimony that Esther was a daughter of God is without dispute, proving that it is possible to be a Christian witness without saying a word. Clearly God demonstrates through Esther the possibility of preaching the Word by using a lifestyle.

The environment in which parents raise children is different from when their parents raised them. That is why so many parents need something that is stable, which will allow them to adjust to environmental changes. The Gospel Model is a stabilizing force and a unity of language, which transcends dialects and the ages. The comprehension and acquisition of the Gospel Model is a Christian education. Nothing else meets the criteria for a Christian education and for this reason a Christian education can be had in the public schools.

Who Should Teach the Gospel Model?

It cannot be over-emphasized that the Gospel Model needs to be part of the Christian common knowledge and language. Christians need to talk it up. Allow parents who are not part of the church community the opportunity to become familiar with the model from the Bible that can save their children. Let parents learn to teach the Gospel Model.

Parents are more motivated to learn new information when they see and hear what it can do for them. By hearing about the many examples of success parents are having with children will make others want familiarity with the Gospel Model. Parents will immediately see the value of using the Gospel Model as an avenue to immunize children against failure in the future. The Gospel Model is the most important ingredient in any Christian education.

It is a pity that Christian parents have little more to say about parenting successes than the secular population has. Perhaps too many Christian parents have not experienced a miracle in their children's lives and that is the reason they are not talking about it The Gospel Model is like a magnifying glass. The magnifier is used to make the really real things more observable. Parents need this type of education. Certain behaviors of children are often overlooked because some behaviors seem insignificant, whereas behaviors viewed through the looking glass of the Gospel Model have an increasing meaning.

In the Bible there is a plethora of information on how one should live, raise, and educate children. When Christian parents cannot quickly pick out this information, doubt creeps in to replace faith as a way of bringing up children. The Gospel

Model helps parents and caretakers of children to correctly view knowledge on how to raise children.

It was the positive statements by the principal that settled the anxieties of the parents of William, Matthew, and Ryan in Quick Success. Notice the difference in Connie as her question took her pastor by surprise, but only because the pastor had previously failed to get the message through to educate her. The *Christian Assertive Effort* is about ways of getting the gospel through to parents who take it to the hearts of children and society.

Christian Education: an Assertive Effort

The Christian elementary schools, high schools, colleges and universities need to take a close look at the reasoning behind the Gospel Model and the *Christian Assertive Effort*. These form the basis for a new curriculum construction and mission statement. It sets a foundation of in-service training for all Christian teachers. In-service training from the Gospel Model is different from in-service training based on the humanistic model. The Gospel Model teaches an absolute God whereas humanism teaches that man is the highest authority for living. Churches can provide in-service training for parents and Christian teachers who attend the public schools. This is a *Christian Assertive Effort* done for parents to protect their children.

It is not easy to teach national values and accept humanism as a substitute for God. Christian teachers in public schools appreciate help. Do not accept the main idea of humanism that education must leave out any of our national values. A secular curriculum is not what the humanist says it is; it is what "we the people" say it is. A presentation of national values can make any secular curriculum a reference to morals that are premised by the authority of an absolute God.

Also, it is entirely possible to think you are teaching the correct religious principles and values to children but are actually teaching a form of humanism, which is opposed to God.

It is equally possible for Christian teachers in the public school domain, while teaching the secular curriculum, to firmly plant the image of Jesus Christ into the hearts of students by using the Gospel Model as a basis for instruction and authority for teaching. The Gospel Model can be silent in words but powerful in demonstration of confidence, feelings of belonging, and in building a vision of Christ. It comes down to what philosophical premises are used as a basis of instruction in morals, religion, psychology, government, and family living.

Gospel Model is Unrestricted in Education

Gospel Model can be global in use. Public educational authorities cannot forbid teachers, guidance counselors, and principals from using the Gospel Model in any area of education. For example, educational guidance counselors, with few exceptions, choose a model for counseling called the non-directive method. This model is considered neutral in the battle between philosophical humanism and an absolute God. But it is not neutral. It allows the student to determine what course to take without any concrete direction. The student is forced to rely on himself void of any values that have not already been provided by parents. Most models in educational counseling are like this. Used on a child like John Walker, the non-directive method is potentially life destructive. If a child has not already accepted God's authority as a premise for decision making, it is likely that humanistic premises will be a bad influence against the traditional family belief in God.

The reasoning for using a non-directive model is that such a model limits the amount of accountability accorded to the guidance counselors. Its underlying goal is to protect the counselor and not to solve the problems of students. This does not take away from the fact that the non-directive method is useful to Christians. In the non-directive approach the counselor mirrors back to the client what the client conveys to the counselor. The client reviews what is mirrored back and makes decisions based on what the client chooses. In this manner many student conflicts are resolved but there are obvious limitations to this method. One being that the client may not be able to figure out the correct decision based on his own information. The Christian counselor is obligated to place the information of the Gospel Model into the counseling event. The humanist counselor would greatly disagree that the counselor should be allowed to assert Christian values into the counseling process even if the client was from a Christian home. With the proper use of the Gospel Model, the Christian teacher or counselor can silently imbed the qualities of the Gospel Model very productively in the counseling process. Expect and be prepared for a counterattack from the forces of humanism. Opposition can happen any time that Christian values are asserted.

Mastery of the Gospel Model well serves both public and private schools. All Christian workers can find guidance in strengthening and immunizing children from failure, as William's principal was able to do for William in Quick Success. My doctor's office provides immunization from the flu each year. The year they did not give me the injection, I had the flu twice. God's immunization works the same way. Counsel children with the Gospel Model and they will be healthier.

Another example of using the Gospel Model in all areas of education is in curriculum construction and presentation. Public schools often change plans of instruction with very few emotional effects on children. A popular plan of teaching in the early 1980's derived its authority from a model found in scientific research. The way words were used, the gestures teachers made, the promptness with which classes began, and the amount of time actually spent on instruction were measured and statistically evaluated to determine the most productive modality of teaching. Called the "Excellence in Education" movement, school principals and curriculum supervisors were required to script everything a teacher did, from where she sat in the room to how many times the teacher used key words in the instructional process.

I saw great value in this instructional plan or model. It really worked well to improve teacher performances and test scores. It seemed to me that the better the principals became at scripting teachers' performances, the better job the teachers did. As we continued to use this model and became better in its use, a new model was being designed to enter the stage of educational reform. Just like pulling the curtain down, the Kentucky Educational Reform Act of 1991 changed everything. Instantly the theme of educational excellence was dropped from the vocabulary of school administrators and teachers. I have not heard the term *educational excellence* used one time by educators in Kentucky since 1991. Kentucky copied this model from other states like California and Florida. I have no doubt that the next reform will render the same devastation as KARA did to the excellence movement.

The point is that most models can be done away with and it will make little difference. Of course, what is suggested here is that the universal missing ingredient is the Gospel Model. The Gospel Model is not an educational reform and the *Christian Assertive Effort* is not a program to be adopted into Christian education. The gospel and the Christian effort are both here to stay. I used the Gospel Model to make all educational models and plans more efficient. This model helped me to zero in on teacher and student needs.

The Gospel Model is on a different and more comprehensive level than most educational and counseling models. There is the Christian way and there are humanistic philosophies. It is possible to be duped into using many or all of the approaches the world makes available, but if Christian and national values are asserted or added to the model, it will make a great difference in the battle for the minds of children in Christ's favor. Teachers who use humanism as an authority for teaching are only teaching. But Christians who incorporate the Gospel Model into all approaches are building on solid rock for Jesus Christ.

Christians have an ulterior motive in teaching: plant the seeds of Jesus Christ into the world. This is, as it should he. Christian education never stops. Initially, the seed is sown in some heart. Next, this seed is multiplied in hearts to appear in communities to become part of a culture, such as the Judeo-Christian culture in America. Satan hates the Christian culture and offers a different scheme, called SINS. There is a part of society that is not going to be won over to Jesus Christ. A very large section of society is committed to humanism. In their lack of knowledge, they think they are right and Christians are wrong (Romans 1:28). Satan's followers are in society in masses, objecting to everything stained with the blood of Christ. Their intent is to calm Christians down so as to slam the door of Christ on society. Satan's model is and always has been humanism. Ignore opposition as much as possible. Keep using the Gospel Model of instruction with all children.

A major battle is going on in public education. God's children are still on the firing line. We do not give up or give in. We keep teaching Christ to our children using the Gospel Model regardless of what society says. Our forefathers continued the struggle from generation to generation until a remnant of children was safe and secure. Our job at the present time is to save the next generation. We can do this.

Childhood Education

There is a season and a time to every purpose under the heaven.
(Ecclesiastes 3:1)

Timing is everything. There is a season for children to be taught, trained, and nurtured. Childhood is that season and a time for learning correct facts (Ecclesiastes 12:1: *Remember now thy Creator in the days of thy youth, while the evil days come not*). Childhood is special. It is the time that the critical, vital, and necessary learning that determines a child's personality is sown. During childhood, parents should be familiar with the Gospel Model to be able to clearly identify the knowledge children will need to be taught.

Parents viewing Christian education through the Gospel Model are building children the same way they would build a house. Childhood is the time the foundation to life is established. A foundation is always built in reference to what the blueprints show the final structure will be like. The entire building will be built according to how the foundation is laid out. Again, timing is everything. Parents can know the whole plan at the time they begin building and teaching a structured foundation.

Parents vitally need the assistance of the educational services of a church to be trained in the use of the Gospel Model. This is intervention on the part of the church because training better parents will create better children, better schools, and better churches. The Gospel Model of learning, guides caretakers of children to know what the behaviors being observed actually mean.

The Gospel Model identifies three domains of a child's mind: the level of self-esteem, the value placed on trying, and goal setting or the lack thereof. By identifying which component of behavior is being observed allows the caretaker of children to respond appropriately with intervention and education to alter children's behavior in a nurturing manner. For example, William, in Quick Success, came to believe he was not smart. He learned to give up and thereby he lost self-esteem. By use of the Gospel Model, the parents saw clearly what were the enabling factors for William.

In Quick Success, William was told that he should be making all "A's." William's self-esteem was enhanced by what he thought adults thought of him. William then showed an interest in getting the job done. His work ethic improved and by the end of the year, William was at the top of his class. See how the Gospel Model is used at the correct time.

In the Bible, King David acquired a reputation that came to be known of by King Saul. David, although a boy, was known as a man of valor. Whereas the heart of King Saul contained a sure bent towards failure, David had been given a pure heart of GOALS. He was well educated, could play the harp and write songs. To sooth his evil spirit, Saul was prompted to inquire concerning David (1 Samuel 16:17).

David was one who had killed a lion and a bear when these attacked his sheep, not a common feat for a grown man, let alone for a boy shepherd. The servants of Saul knew of David. This is typical of personalities of GOALS. The automatic response to success came natural to David. It was the way he had been educated and people knew it.

Later, when the giant Goliath said that the army of Israel was like rats that hid in holes in the ground, the army believed the giant. When the giant made fun of the army of Israel, the men were in great fear and trembled. But David said, *who is this uncircumcised Philistine, that he should defy the armies of the living God?* This was a different attitude and not one of defeat (1 Samuel 17:26).

David possessed a different response and a different mindset, separate from the one the army of Israel had. The army of Israel believed whatever the giant said about them was true. Can you see how David had an adaptive explanatory lifestyle and his Hebrew brothers had a maladaptive lifestyle?

David's brother heard him speaking up against the giant and rebuked David. But David killed the giant anyway. David knew who he was, that he was the anointed child of God. David believed the power within him (the personality of GOALS) was greater than the obstacles that were in this world. David was ready to change a society of fear into a world of hope. Parents can instill in the hearts of their children a belief that they can overcome obstacles. Children can possess a unique personality regardless of the school they attend.

Christian Education for Adults

David was not yet an adult but adults could have used his valor. David faced the giant while adults hid. After David killed the giant, the adults began to have faith in their God. You might say they were converted to their own religion. Just as there is a season for children to grasp the Gospel Model, for adults who have not yet done so, there is good reason to change their adult minds and way of thinking. But, to do this, accept the Gospel, repent, and walk in the light. Many adults today need to be converted to their own religious beliefs. Believing parents provide the best education for children. An assertive faith puts parents in the household of God. In the Epistle of Hebrews a list is given of the many men and women with an active faith who all had a fruitful and productive life because of their childhood and adult style of living. Each in turn had to educate their children. Read the eleventh chapter of Hebrews with an open mind and you will see how the Gospel Model works to educate adults as well as children.

Most everyone on the list had moments of failure and occasional conflict with God's ways but in the end, the Gospel Model was strong enough to place followers into God's hall of fame. To Paul the list represented the household of God. All were men or women who acted on faith within the Gospel Model and saw things in a different light from the rest of society. Learning about God as a child will have this type of affect on children and will result in the creation of great adults. You are what you do. If you kill giants, you are a giant killer. If you protect sheep, you are a good shepherd. If you hide in a hole, you're a rat.

In David's time adult armies of Israel were trained and conditioned by their enemy to believe that no matter what they did, the army of Goliath would win the battle. They saw themselves as the giant saw them, as rats to hide in holes. They were frozen, sore afraid to act. They did not realize, if they acted on faith, the world conditions would change. Fortunately for them, David, the young shepherd boy, knew from experience that this situation could be changed by the power of a clean heart. Are you beginning to see how the Gospel Model works?

> But without faith it is impossible to please him: for he that cometh to God must believe that he is, and that he is a rewarder of them that diligently seek him. (Hebrews 11:6)

Adults cannot overcome the world while digging holes in which to hide. A student will never aspire to be a doctor if he views the learning of math and science as too difficult an obstacle to overcome. It will not matter what school he attends. Think about the power you have over the lives of children while asserting the Gospel Model by adopting GOALS in your adult life. Physical harm may threaten you but you will have the staff of Christ upon which to lean provided you wrestle with God's plan.

CHAPTER TWELVE

Joined at the Hip of Jacob

By faith Jacob, when he was a dying, blessed both the sons of Joseph; and worshipped, leaning upon the top of his staff. (Hebrews 11:21)

The *Christian Assertive Effort* is God's plan to place Christian values back into the American culture and society. When Jacob died he was standing and worshipping God. The main reason Jacob was leaning on his staff at the end was that God had blessed him in his hip and weakened him there. Since that time Jacob had to depend on his staff for support the remainder of his life. The staff was a type of Christ the Gospel Model. Jacob, when he died, was still active in faith, still standing on the model of Christ and blessing his descendents. Jacob asserted his faith until the very end.

The Gospel Model must still be asserted. Assertive is the key word. We take our spiritual weapons, our values, all revealed in the Gospel Model, and place these into service for our Lord and Savior, Jesus Christ. Parents and caretakers of children simultaneously assert the model of God into the hearts of children through an educational process. In the previous chapter, David's parents had asserted into David's heart the Gospel Model, and you could easily identify that it was part of his lifestyle. David certainly was not one to give up easily. Although David went astray, the Bible Model had him harnessed, and he came back to God.

There are two target areas for the Gospel Model. The primary target area is spread out over a world domain called society. In the Bible the world is a reference to society. When Jesus said to go into the entire world to teach the gospel, He meant that the message must be taken to all of society. Secondly, an important target area is found in the heart of children. What makes up the target area? The target area of children and society is made up of conditioned or trained beliefs called mindsets. The world has a heart and so do children. Societal values are stored in the hearts of schools, religion, philosophy, law, communities, churches, and nations. The categories or branches of society are extensive. When Christians train and condition the world to accept Christian values, Christians are taking the Gospel Model to the heart of society.

Humanism is the model Satan uses to oppose God. Humanism is any philosophy that places man at the top of the moral or spiritual order in determining what is proper human behavior. Humanism is the philosophic antithesis of absolute God or Being. Humanism is that spirit of anti-Christ referred to by John (2 John 1:7). The absolute Being theory is the basis from which most democratic governments derive their authority to govern. Humanism is represented by such concepts as moral relativity, freedom of choice, the use of recreational drugs, sex, and totally free thought. Humanism, the belief that man creates all gods, is the enemy of orthodox Christianity. Man is his own moral authority. Humanism seeks to condition society to automatically respond by this philosophy. That is the reason Christ said Christians were not one with society (John 15:19).

The Hip of Jacob

The Christian Assertive Effort and *Raising Children the Bible Way* are two concepts that are joined at the hip of Jacob. *The Christian Assertive Effort* is not a program to be adopted and then forgotten, but an effort that Christians make continuously. The Gospel Model of behavior and God's way of raising children is the Word of God and dictates the things Christians must do to spread the gospel. *The Christian Assertive Effort* and *Raising Children the Bible Way* are not programs except in the sense that the church is programmed to teach the word of God.

The Christian effort is the church testifying to God's Word as it actively asserts Christian values into society. This has always been God's one and only program of salvation. This testimony has not changed and God's people must not give up on this model as if it were a program to be accepted or rejected. To not make an effort for Christ is to reject salvation.

Christians are to infiltrate all parts of society. Be in the schools, government, clubs, charities, and community activities, and always planting the word. We are the light of the society of America. Without our influence society has lost its godly flavor. Without the Christian's influence society is of little value according to Jesus. In Matthew 5:13 Jesus tells us that when society follows humanism, it will become a shambles. Christians make society better.

The devil can only take control of society when Christians give up. All we have to do is *not* give in, to stand still and wait out the philosophies of men and die like Jacob, standing on Christ. The history of humanism has been that of failure. Standing firm will protect our Christian values. Standing up and being counted will be enough.

Jews have been spread out all over the world. They have not been conquerors but are known rather as the persecuted ones. They, however, have had an active faith and have stood the test of time. All their historical enemies are dead and I think they will outlive their modern enemies too.

What is wrong with society? Why has American education taken the route of humanism and freedom of expression for everyone except the believers in God? We do not have to be silent. The act of asserting the Christian philosophy and its value system into society is something Christians do as a result of having been touched by God. It is how they stand.

When Jacob was blessed of God after having wrestled with the angel of the Lord until light began to appear, the Lord changed Jacob by touching him at the hip (Genesis 32:24–25). The Lord blessed Jacob with children who were to serve God and thereby assert godly values into the world by being known by society as God's people. The children of Jacob became a great nation named Israel and became an example, pattern, and model to society to enable the peoples of society to know and understand God (Genesis 32:28). God used Israel to enlighten the worldwide society. For this same reason God has left the church in the world to plant or assert the Word of God so society can see its way back to God (Matthew 5:14). The model of turning people back to God was determined from the time God created the world (2 Thessalonians 2:13).

We do not see the Gospel Model clearly in Jacob until God touched Jacob, at which time Jacob's name was changed to Israel. In the Bible, Israel is a type of the church, because Israel became known to the world as the people of God. Through both Israel and the church, God intended to save mankind by preserving in man and in the church the image or model of God (2 Timothy 4:18). This is what it means to be a Christian and a member of the church of God. You are an instrument of God to enlighten the world.

Until teachers and counselors begin to make lesson plans on the basis of belief in an absolute God, schools will not see the light. Politicians and lawyers must practice their professions with a belief in absolute law. Just be in society to remind the world that God is not dead. However, God might just as well be dead if we do not present Him to society.

In the Second Epistle to the Thessalonians, chapter two, the apostle Paul warns the church of the destructive nature of humanism. There can be no doubt that Paul considered humanism to be the antichrist. In one of the last verses of this chapter, Paul tells the church how to defeat humanism and how to make the testimony of Jesus Christ strong in society. *Therefore, brethren, stand fast, and hold the traditions which ye have been taught, whether by word, or our epistle* (verse 15). Christians must do what Christians do.

An unconverted society will view the assertive church as a nuisance. The concept of God touching us and changing us is important in the scenario of God. Assertiveness, which sometimes brings conflict, is the behavior God wants from the church and parents in order to slap down humanism. The placing of God's value system into society changes society, making the world better for our children. This is a conditioning process that only Christians can begin.

Society has quietly accepted humanism as its model. The model of God starts with His people who are called by His name advancing the cause of Christ. His people must deliberately place the model of God into the hearts of their children. A substitute model will not do. To be Christian, it must be the real model of God. This eliminates any humanistic model. Jesus Christ was talking about humanism when he told his disciples that they could not love both God and man (Matthew 6:24).

Christians must know and be aware that idolatry today is the honoring, worshipping, or giving respect to any philosophy other than that of almighty God. When man worshiped God under the laws of Moses, it was the worshipping of carved images of stone and metal that God warned His people to avoid. In worshipping God today, we worship with spirit and mind. The idols of modern times are ideas and philosophies that turn us away from God. *Beware lest any man spoil you through philosophy and vain deceit, after the tradition of men, after the rudiments of the world, and not after Christ* (Colossians 2:8).

Society belongs to the devil and he has found ways within society to try to neutralize and stifle the message of God. The idols of the devil today are false philosophies and the moral behavior that emanates from these false philosophies. A false idol is any mental image or model that denies the value system of Jesus Christ. Satan, tempting Jesus, said for Jesus to fall down and worship him or his image. The devil showed Jesus all the wonders of the world and said Jesus could have all these things (Matthew 4). In the four gospels, whenever Jesus was tempted, He was always tempted with a great idea of what Satan could give Him. But Jesus knew that the gifts of the devil's philosophy were designed to destroy the soul. The Great Model of God was Jesus Christ, the restorer of the soul.

Christians must not be calmed down or duped by society. Society belongs to the devil and his moral philosophy comes from humanism. Humanism is subtle and urges Christians to not be so radical or assertive. The fact is that anything the Christian does is branded by humanism as being radical, illogical, and extreme.

Humanism in society does not want a Christian prayer given in public forums; therefore, society has made the substitution of a humanistic prayer called "a moment of silence." Here again this prayer is like the prayer that Shadrach, Meshach, and Abed-nego were ordered to pray in the third chapter of the Book of Daniel. Shadrach, Meshach, and Abed-nego would not kneel and give respect to another god or philosophy, but chose to be thrown into a fiery furnace. When we tolerate this humanistic prayer and other sly efforts of humanism, how close are we coming to violating the commandment of having "no other gods"? Is not humanism having its way with us? Should we give honor and respect to "no specific god"? Might this moment of silence be a small, little move away from the Christian God? I have often observed this moment of silence and I have always known to whom to pray. But others, I am not so sure about. Are others getting the message that it is okay to pray to any god just as long as you pray? If so, this is not what God intended from the church of Jesus Christ. I look forward to the time that an audience is asked to stand and observe a moment of silence and every Christian in the audience begins by praying the Lord's Prayer. Christians, like Paul, really did *know in whom they believed.* They refused to give in or acquiesce to any philosophy that took them in the slightest direction away from God.

The definition of the Gospel Model of behavior is different from the models society uses. God's model begins with who God really is. He is not some unspecific entity. And this specific God is the only image man is to follow. We are not Jacob, but Israel. The name Jacob means deceit. We are deceived in thinking man is equal to God, as do many false beliefs (humanism). By touching us, God changes our ways of thinking. This change makes us Israel or the church. In the Gospel Model we are what we think and do. We are smart because we study to show ourselves intelligent (2 Timothy 2:15). We are right in our point of view because we worked things out correctly in our minds by yielding our minds to Christ. Making a Christian effort is not a program of propaganda but a way of life, a natural responding of Christian faith. That is what being intelligent is.

I believe and have learned that anything that can be taught can be learned. Math and science are not difficult to learn although many think otherwise. These people who think otherwise never become doctors or scientists. The secret to learning math and science is making your mind receptive to the laws of math and science and being willing to study by these laws. In this same way, we can both learn and teach society to serve God. In the model of God, people change society in order to overcome it. The world is not static and can be made to fit God's plan. God's people, with a little faith, can move mountains to make society like they want it to be.

Since Christians can affect the world or society, it is safe and inviting to establish high and lofty goals (Philippians 4:13: *I can do all things through Christ which strengtheneth me*). In the model of God, goals motivate us to action. Christian assertiveness on society moves Christ into the world with His message.

The Assertion of the Philosophy of Christ

The assertion of Christian values and philosophy has always had an enemy, which has always opposed the theory of an absolute God and Creator. The enemy has been and still is the moral philosophies of man, called humanism, which has made a strong appearance of late in our nation's government and educational systems.

The *Christian Assertive Effort* seeks to re-establish the concrete and absolute standards of law that are uniquely characteristic of the Constitution of the United States, the Declaration of Independence, and the Bill of Rights. These absolute standards of behavior are in opposition to humanistic philosophical positions. It is an absolute Creator to which Americans overwhelmingly cling and which provides our moral resolve and determination.

In the Constitution of the United States, the Declaration of Independence and the Bill of Rights, God is described as the absolute being that created man, moral laws, and unalienable rights. Notice that an absolute God created a law that governs man. Man and government both are under the rule of God in God's plans and in the Constitution. Our national documents define what is righteous behavior and what is evil behavior. These documents of law state the philosophical position of the United States.

Both God and the devil have planed a way for man to behave. Our Lord Jesus Christ is the Gospel Model of good while our enemy the devil is the ultimate model of evil. The devil's model is subtle and not easily identified as evil, because it is very much like the Gospel Model of good. The devil's model places man as the highest moral standard in the universe.

Many adopt humanism as an appropriate model of life simply because they have not given much thought to the philosophy of humanism. The following fact cannot be emphasized too often. Humanism is very much like the Judeo-Christian model of behavior. The similarity is due to the fact that humanity was made in the image of God; thus, humanism only differs from God's model in that man replaces God as the standard giver of morality. This is just as it was in the Garden of Eden when man wanted to be like God.

The evil of any humanistic approach first appears harmless until its damage is done and great atrocities have occurred. The slaughter of seven million Jews by Germany took place after the Nazis prepared the German society to accept humanism. The slaughter of the Jews required that a whole nation accept first the concept that killing Jews was the moral thing to do. Nazism claimed that man, not God, was responsible to say what was moral. The Germans believed it was a showing of courage when they enforced their law upon the world. The humanistic philosophy of Nazism was in direct contrast to the Christian model of morality and democracy. People abandoning their absolute faith in God allowed the growth of Nazism. Christians today must not abandon their belief in the absolute God, but must make a stand.

The humanist converts flourish quietly during times of peace and prosperity. During this time they preach the superiority of man and affirm that man should be freed from absolute law. Humanism allows its followers the freedom to do whatever they desire, even to the point of national anarchy.

America's national documents reject this point of view or else there would never be any order in our Judeo-Christian society. Once before in American history, the American people had to reject anarchy as a political force in favor of absolute law. The followers of this extreme humanist movement were called *anarchist* and worked towards the collapse of all government. There has to be order for society to function. Choosing absolute standards has always been the decision of democratic states.

I tell you the truth, Americans have never chosen to follow the tenants of humanism or to be governed by its precepts. Yet, the move is on to assert this model and to disallow Americans to assert the Judeo-Christian value system in modern society. Look at American society and how it changes. Historically, American citizens gave government the power to decide issues of morality by the standards laid down by the absolute God. These laws were protected by the Constitution of the United States.

The humanist's cry for freedom decays society's traditional order. The right of women to have an abortion is humanistic. This belief is inherent to the humanistic philosophy of moral relativity. The person's right to choose what is moral is humanism. Advocates of alternative sexual behavior follow the tenants of humanism. Man shows courage when he makes decisions based on what he chooses to be moral, so say the humanist and the Nazis. Man should be free to choose sex, drugs, and a lifestyle of his own choosing whether or not these choices cut across the value system of most Americans. That is what the humanists are saying and doing.

Nazi Germany is an example of what happens to a nation when citizens free themselves from God to establish their own moral standards. Starting at the end of World War I, the Germans began to accept the tenets of Nazism. The dangerously evil results of Nazism were not apparent to the world until this form of humanism had its greatest successes in hand. The evil of humanism was not apparent. Many Germans did not see it until the collapse of the Nazi government at the end of World War II. By this time their country was in waste. The devil's model of behavior has always been a subtle force called humanism that has led to chaos.

Our nation's best known slogans make it clear that Americans stand with God and absolute law. The framers of our country recognized the dangers of moral relativity. Our founding fathers made it clear that we were "one nation under God," that "all men were *created* equal," and that the belief in an absolute God was accepted by "we the people" saying that "In God we trust."

The U.S.A. had a relatively long time of peace just before the 9–11 attack on the New York Trade Center. The grip that humanism then had on our nation was rejected by the instincts of a predominately Christian nation. Since 9–11 there has been a religious revival taking place and a return of conservative beliefs with God as the absolute moral authority in our country. Liberal proponents of humanism seem less harsh on fundamental Christian beliefs at this time, but they are only laying low until the wave of nationalism passes. The United States must never succumb to any type of humanistic point of view. The time is right for Christians to assert the Gospel Model of Christ into our culture.

Patriotic Duty

Far too long now Christians have allowed humanism to speak loudly in our public schools to the point that the values of the majority are not heard. The assertion of Christ-like values by teachers and parents into society is a patriotic duty. The rejection of humanism is the moral thing to do. We must find the courage to do so. Parents and schools do have the obligation as well as the moral authority to say what lifestyles should be allowed and taught in our schools. The fight for God's absolute authority begins with each person in each local community. That is the reason the *Christian Assertive Effort* begins with *Raising Children the Bible Way.*

The public schools refuse to teach creationism, even though our Constitution says that God created man. The Constitution of the U.S.A. makes this concept a political belief as well as a religious point of view. Public schools should be required to teach the creationist's position, not because it defeats the theory of evolution, but because creationism is part of the adopted philosophy of our nation. Humanism has no basis on which to enforce its beliefs on Americans.

Few limitations, however, are placed on teaching the evolutionary concepts, although the Constitution rejects the survival of the fittest theory. Humanism and evolution are racist philosophies. It is from the theory of evolution that the Nazis derived their authority to kill the Jews. The KKK and other racist organizations say their race is superior to other races. For this reason the rights of black people have been denied for centuries. Thankfully, the absolute God still agrees that all men were created equal.

It is a fact that teachers who do not accept humanism as a valid philosophy are duped into following humanistic models of teaching in the name of democracy and individual freedom. It is the right of American teachers to reject the humanistic philosophy, more so than it is the right of humanists to block the public expression of God's point of view. At least God is Constitutional.

Although we cannot ask schools to teach any particular religion, we can ask them, and it seems we should be able to require them, to teach America's political values. It seems that

Christians should be duty bound to bring to the classroom the values of the community they serve. Christian teachers can be assisted by the church to discover ways and methods of exposing students and parents to a wider view of our absolute and national value system. It is within the professional duty of principals and teachers to refer parents to outside agencies that teach absolute values that can be used for training children and that have not been contaminated with a philosophical system of humanism.

Citizens are duty bound to require schools to publish copies of their educational philosophy. A parental right of review is rarely questioned. Schools can be required, if we make it so, to offer alternative value systems if theirs differ from the value system of the community, especially when the belief in absolute value is the basis of our national government.

The silent use of humanism, which constitutes the imposing of an arbitrary value system upon children, can be uncloaked. Parents must not only be free to say what values children will be taught but also free to choose for their children the value system used by their schools. It is as fair for citizens to reject humanism as it is for humanistic citizens to reject theories of the absolute. If public schools really want to please parents and citizens, we need them to be aware of what we want. After schools have disclosed their philosophic position, and if it is a humanistic position, we must require them to make available to students the offering of an alternative value system. The alternative value system must be like that found in the Constitution of the United States.

The church and Christians in their demands must *not* be in opposition to schools. Chances are, there are more Christians working in schools than humanists and they will welcome our assertive attitude. We must encourage the public schools to call upon us for counseling and guidance in clarifying what absolute Christian values are. The workers in the public domain are no more pleased with being trapped and duped by humanism than the strongest Christian believer.

The church must train its members in the Gospel Model of behavior in raising children, for this model is the Word of God. The church has been the harbor of Christian values, but now it is time to assert these values into society. In actuality, humanism should be viewed as the alternative point of view and God's absolute moral philosophy should be viewed as the mainstay of our schools and government.

A Beginning

The asserting of Christian values back into the culture begins with parents. The Gospel Model of living began with parents when God created Adam and Eve with instructions to subdue the earth and to multiply after their gender. The devil also presented his model of behavior, which was humanism. The devil's presentation to Adam and Eve was close to the Gospel Model in that the devil promised mankind that he could become as God. The devil says that mankind will prosper and be like gods by following his model. But God said man would surely die by following humanism.

Cultures and civilizations that depended on various forms of humanism have perished. It is no accident that the nation of Israel still exists. Communism, which denounces God but praises man, has failed. The USSR lost the Cold War because it could not stand up to the belief in the absolute God. When the USSR was branded as an evil empire it was uncloaked and perished from the face of the earth.

The assertion of Christian values begins with parents bringing up children by the Gospel Model, which will uncloak evil and save our civilization. The *Christian Assertive Effort* directs parents to persuade schoolteachers and educators to provide alternative philosophical approaches to humanism. Do not attack schools, but work cooperatively with them and at the same time uncloak their humanistic tendencies that they themselves may not see. *Raising Children the Bible Way* can provide the initial insight into the biblical model of behavior.

As we get our foot back in the door, it is possible to require public school teachers to write into individual instructional plans the values parents want children to know. The Constitutional beliefs in an absolute God, a creator of equal people, the rule of God's authority, the trusting in God, all these beliefs add up to a great moral nation and a basis for teaching. "We the people" of the Constitution attest to this fact. The highest law in the land is saying that its value system is to be taught and to be passed on to the generations that follow.

The Christian Assertive Effort

The main contribution of *Raising Children the Bible Way* is that it delineates clearly what God's model of behavior is. The Gospel Model must be followed by Christians and planted into society for the following three reasons. First, the Gospel Model must be used to protect the Christian faith. Two points of view in the universe are in conflict and at war with each other. The belief in an absolute God versus humanism is on the line. Humanism and unbelief are the same, are subtle, and sometimes come cloaked in a disguise to appear harmless. It always adheres to an underlying evil principle that one cannot really know God and ultimately must depend on man's wisdom in moral decisions. Humanism has made a strong appearance in society with its foremost-cloaked goal to raise children by the tenets of humanism in the name of religious freedom.

To save the Christian culture in America, a model of behavior that is generic to the Bible must be used to raise children. Humanism must be cast out, in all of its subtle forms, its premises uncloaked, and the Gospel Model asserted to replace it. Our Bible teaches us that Christians are to take the gospel into society, thus the public schools. It is not enough to build Christian private schools, although this is worth doing, but the public schools must have the Gospel Model at least as an equal force to humanism. In any intellectual conflict between humanism and the absolute God, in philosophy, in religion, or civic ingenuity, the Bible philosophy will not only stand its ground but also will ultimately win. And if society deems it unfair to support the tenets of the Judeo-Christian culture in the public domain, humanism must be forbidden an audience there also. Humanism is as much a religious belief as Christianity and should not be accorded any special honor.

It is our duty to force a conflict between the absolute God and humanism. To do this Christians need only to oppose rule and regulation making using the tenets of humanism. Do not allow schools and government boards to make rules based on humanistic philosophies, which do not deserve a place of honor. Only absolute values are honored by the Constitution.

Assertive Christians must make appearances before boards of education to demand the premises of decision making agree with the majority of the community, not with a few humanist renegades who have ceased unlawful control of the decision-making process. Renegade is a good term to apply to humanism, which threatens to deprive Americans of what they value the most and replace it with a false belief.

Secondly, it is important that every Christian is familiar and knowledgeable as to what Christian-American beliefs are. These are all found in the Gospel Model of behavior. Yes, we believe in religious freedom. But most of all, we believe in freedom for Christians to use the premises of their beliefs in public life. Go armed into the public to do battle with the weapons of warfare.

For the weapons of our warfare are not carnal, but mighty through God to the pulling down of strong holds. (2 Corinthians 10:4)

Humanism has a strong hold on America and is trying to shape the culture to fit its image. Listen to what Peter had to say in regards to humanism: *But sanctify the Lord God in your hearts: and be ready always to give an answer to every man that asketh you a reason of the hope that is in you with meekness and fear* (1 Peter 3:15). Paul said this type of reasoning was strong for those who exercised this knowledge, which they possess in their hearts (Hebrews 5:14). Learn this model. It is generic to the Word of God and the Constitution of the U.S.A.

Thirdly, use the Gospel Model in your personal life. Train children by the Gospel Model by living your beliefs. Own the Gospel Model as your own personal philosophy of life. Join with others who share your beliefs. Insist that teachers not be allowed to substitute other values for your Christian beliefs. Humanism will not do as a premise for decision making. Show how powerful the Gospel Model is by saving families and children that are at risk. Lead, do not follow. Begin a group in your church or community for the sole purpose of learning the Gospel Model of behavior. Address the PTA, school boards, and community meetings with the idea that America is a Judeo-Christian community and that citizens would rather use Christian premises of the community to shape beliefs. Forbid the use of humanism as a premise for decision making.

CHAPTER THIRTEEN

Here's Dr. Larry

But what saith the answer of God unto him? I have reserved to myself seven thousand men, who have not bowed the knee to the image of Baal. (Romans 11:4)

When the man of God thought he was alone and prayed to God, "Why?", the Lord said that seven thousand men in the neighborhood were ready to stand with the man of God. Dr. Larry Bush was one of those seven thousand for me. He took a look at what God was showing me and immediately sensed the Holy Spirit and quickly adopted the Gospel Model as his own. Together we came up with several great ideas for an assertive effort by the church. His biggest contribution to me was his ability to organize and correctly name components of the Gospel Model. The terminology of GOALS and SINS was most helpful.

Dr. Larry Bush was my pastor. When he was introduced to the concept of the Gospel Model, he insisted that I train him to use it. He had a doctorate from Colorado State University in the field of science and a master's in theology.

"Teach me," he said.

For our first session, Dr. Larry invited me to his house. The basic concept had already been explained, which fired his enthusiasm. He needed to have it demonstrated to him. We did some role-playing where Dr. Larry played a frustrated parent and also a frustrated and disorderly child. What surprised me was that once Dr. Larry grasped the formula of "what I am is what I do" that, "what I do changes things," and "goals and purpose holds everything together", the model seemed to do the rest of the orientation. The Gospel Model was didactic, self-perpetuating, growing on its own power and creating new knowledge. The Gospel Model itself had such training power of its own.

So, here are Dr. Larry's notes from our first session.

KIDS IN TROUBLE—BASED ON INFORMATION FROM BILL SCOTT, ASHLAND, KY; APRIL 2002.

Kids in trouble could be your kids or my grandkids. It is a well-known fact that teachers can pick out of a class those students who will most likely be good students and those who are most likely to fail. What is it about those failing children that jumps out to experienced teachers? Studies have shown that both subjective and objective criteria leads to the conclusion those kids can be picked out on the basis of how they respond to life events.

These life experiences (lifestyles) lead a child to respond in one of two ways.

1. ADAPTIVE: "GOOD" (POSITIVE SELF-ESTEEM) optimistic
2. MALADAPTIVE: "BAD" (NEGATIVE SELF-ESTEEM) PESSIMISTIC

Which is dominant determines a child's response to life situations and determines the emotional damage done. No one is either totally good or bad, but a mixture. The goal is to improve and reinforce the good, or adaptive life style, and limit the bad or maladaptive life style. This is to be done largely through use of positive reinforcement at all levels.

While failures can be picked out, should a teacher/parent/ concerned Christian just stand by and let them fail? We must do something to change the course of their lives!

We all want to allow a child to grow healthy (Jesus came healing). When we ask, "Why do children fail," it is apparent that their life style is key. In addition, we understand that we all learn from early infanthood from words. This leads to the logical conclusion that what a child says can identify that child as a failure or a success (note that Jesus is the "WORD," the "LIFE," the "WAY," not a success or failure, health or sickness (?)

The problem we can see in unsuccessful "failures" did not happen overnight and cannot be corrected immediately. Yet, correction can be rapid and lasting. Failure comes in many areas with a lack of positive reinforcement, which results in a poor self-image. This works out with students who hate school, homework, study, etc. and consequently do poorly and live up to their expectations of themselves!

The course of correction must determine and return to the first sense of failure and teach success by changing that ineffective lifestyle. It will take work, but the process WORKS!

Basically the process simply uses positive words and actions. The parents hold the keys here. The parent, however, is not totally alone out on a limb but will be provided resources to help them

PARENT (or "REPARENT") along with other family and friend relationships.

Underlying the process is the reality that keeping the desired goal in mind, helps to reinforce positive actions. "You are what You do!" If a parent is maladaptive—responds in improper ways to life situations—the child will do the same . The reverse is the same, so why not do it right?

The strategy for a child needs to be developed individually for that child. It should be maintained all through the educative and growing—maturing process, from elementary school through high school and into college as much as possible. The younger the child is, the easier it will be to change the life style. This is because the process is like building a mold. The mold here is to form words in a positive manner and make it part of who the person is. The perfect mold we can use as a model is Jesus Christ, the divine word of God who formed the world from the heart. If we see an imperfect and defective statue, we know it came from an imperfect and defective mold. The Bible tells us that good and bad come out of the mouth from the heart. Success is not only possible, but expected when we allow our changed hearts to focus on the best successful model.

In human relationships, control is a central practical issue. Who is in control—parents or child? Is it a choice of force or kindness? No! Unfortunately, a core problem with maladaptive parents and children, is they are looking for love in all the wrong places and ways. Tough love does what is needed because it recognizes that weakness in staying the course will always result in a shipwreck and that is the very thing we are trying to correct and avoid. It is a well-known fact that parents are the prime influences in a child's life and influences their behaviors over all other relationships from peers to teachers. This is particularly true in the middle childhood years.

Now that you see that there is hope, practice it at home. Yes, it will take time, but the young learn and change quickly. Parent power involves changing parents as they change their minds. You can do it! There has not been a failure yet. With the right attitude, do you have the courage to try it? If you wanted to change the world, you can do it one heart at a time. A small seed of positive reinforcement acts like planting a tiny mustard seed, which grows into a large bush.

When success happens, ever the littlest of them celebrate with gist! There is the right way (God's way) or 1000's of other ways (devil's ways). For the church, we must realize that the goal is not the extremes of adaptive or maladaptive life styles, but be united in attaining the maximum positive goal. In this way each person does his or her thing, but by bringing them together in the positive atmosphere of the church body. We all can help each other build strong self-esteem as we surrender our lives and those of our children to the one who created us. God sent His son to redeem us from the life style which destroys to a life style that offers His Holy Spirit to maintain the positive and hope of a continued good life.

CHAPTER FOURTEEN

Notes, Handbooks and Manuals

Developing a manual for the Gospel Model and the *Christian Assertive Effort* is something you do. The primary purpose for taking notes and building a manual/handbook is to organize in your mind just exactly how the Gospel Model is dynamically driven. The Gospel Model is a new concept for you and God wants you to be successful in its use. Therefore, creating a manual and taking notes will really help you understand what you are learning.

A manual is a special handbook because it is a history of workable actions enabling its user to *do* things correctly. Teachers, accountants, managers, and all sorts of professionals use manuals and handbooks. A manual begins by informing the user how a specific machine or program operates. Handouts, notes, and new learning can be added and used to guide future behavior.

Using Christ correctly results in the *Christian Assertive Effort,* which is joined at the hip of Jacob (or at the point of God's blessing). As you study your Bible and live the lifestyle of the *Christian Assertive Effort,* make notes, whether mental or written, of the things you learn about a Christian lifestyle. You can write in the margins in your Bible or on a separate notebook. But keep track of your growth.

By understanding the psychological dynamics of behavior through the Gospel Model, a greater measure of control over behavior is earned. Jesus Christ viewed behavior as a response to intellectual and philosophical acceptance of His teachings. Learning an intellectual explanation of Christ will enhance the utilization of the Gospel Model to the fullest. A manual tells what performances are needed to make a dynamic machine work well. The intellectual knowing about the Gospel Model motivates Christians to make actions better. What one believes to be true has everything to do with behavior. Do you believe Christ is our example and model?

Belief greatly influences behavior. How you spend your money, how you raise your children, where you live, and how you sojourn among men are all motivated by intellectual beliefs of what is really real. The Gospel Model teaches the way for the fullest utilization of a Christian lifestyle in determining planned behavior.

Awareness of Christian beliefs provides a way of doing things. To understand God, Moses was commanded to write and make books, laws, and models for directions to bring the children of Israel to maturity. Moses' writings, called the *Torah*, are outlines of how God wanted people to live, and contained all the laws of God. The *Talmud*, written later, was a handbook and commentary that explained what the *Torah* and tradition was saying to the Jewish people.

A greater model in the appearing of Christ replaced the Law of Moses. The patterns, symbols, and examples in the Jewish law were all models to help Israel to a spiritual reality in which mankind had been cast. Stories, images, patterns and models, were meant to convey tremendous knowledge about the eternal world that God inhabits. It is through these models, especially the model of Christ, that God has chosen to share eternity with us.

> For thus saith the high and lofty One that inhabiteth eternity, whose name is Holy; I dwell in the high and holy place, with him also that is of a contrite and humble spirit, to revive the spirit of the humble, and to revive the heart of the contrite ones. (Isaiah 57:15)

Models, patterns, and images are meant to bring us to God, therefore, to eternity. Christ is the greatest model of time and He is our link to the Eternal One. When we accepted the eternal model of Jesus Christ, we entered the realm of the eternal where God is. Since God is a verb, it is required that action, the doing, be that which brings one into the presence of God. Action is the only way to share spiritual communion with God. In essence, God is still allowing His people to come close to Him by manual instruction for their actions. Christ as a model is always dynamic. If you are not doing something for God, manual knowledge points out that there is a breakdown in how you serve God. The knowledge you learn from using the Gospel Model will serve you well in the future and enable you to fix broken parts.

Christians who do not understand how to be a Christian are confused about what Christ is and what He said to mankind. Using Christ as a model one learns how to be a Christian. The Gospel Model is self-perpetuating in teaching important information that will help you follow Christ. Improve your life with new learning and with each epiphany God gives you.

Preparing a manual is like taking notes in a classroom. Through high school and college, those who took the best notes generally received the best grades. King David and the prophet Jeremiah took notes of life and their handbook was put forth in the form of written songs. Take note of the following verses.

For I acknowledge my transgressions: and my sin is ever before me.
(Psalm 51:3)

In all thy ways acknowledge him, and he shall direct thy paths.
(Proverbs 3:6)

*We acknowledge, O LORD, our wickedness, and the iniquity of our
fathers: for we have sinned against thee.* (Jeremiah 14:20)

King David kept track of his sins. By noting his mistakes
and with God's presence to help him see the *way*, David had
each step he took directed by God. The prophet Jeremiah took
note of the fact that both he and his fathers had sinned and like
David, he was always aware of his past sins. The reason was
that Jeremiah did not want to repeat his sins. They used the
knowledge of past mistakes to strengthen their moral and spiritual life with God. Keeping track of what God shows you will
strengthen you.

The idea of *government* is a model. *Communism* is a model of
government. The former USSR decided to junk the model that
governed their lives because it did not work. The idea of God is
an action model and He really works. Any ideas you have about
God that do not work need to be abandoned.

Although there are no perfect bodies, the perfect, physical,
functioning human body is the model that is used in all schools
of medicine in which doctors are trained. Again, it is not likely
that a perfect human body can be found anywhere. But future
doctors study a perfect body to learn what can go wrong with
the body that leads to poor health and death. A Christian's
perfect model is Christ. The Bible also often uses the analogy
of a body to explain spiritual health. The Bible is what we have
as our manual; it is about a perfect God and begins with a perfect man created by God to live a perfect *way*.

Some doctors are better than others and some preachers are better at correctly dividing the word of God (2 Timothy 2:15). Use a strict biblical logic with the Gospel Model. Science has a strict logic to which it must adhere, called the scientific method. The truth of scientific reality is evaluated by how well the rules of the scientific model have been followed to explain truth. Christians also have a scientific and spiritual method in order to arrive at the truth. One rule is that Christians must study. Properly done, a manual knowledge of the Gospel Model will differentiate between you and humanism.

Something peculiar and different is seen in the main characters in the Bible who reasoned about God's *way*. This peculiar quality was passed from fathers to sons that made sons great fathers. If parents can identify and capture this quality and pass it on to their children, they, in turn, can create well-adjusted children, able themselves to become great parents and thinkers on God.

Finally, brethren, whatsoever things are true, whatsoever things are honest, whatsoever things are just, whatsoever things are pure, whatsoever things are lovely, whatsoever things are of good report; if there be any virtue, and if there be any praise, think on these things. (Philippians 4:8)

The Bible teaches that your life is an open book. You are developing your own personal manual and handbook (2 Corinthians 3:21). Begin early in life to catalog into your book the experiences that have assisted you and others in using the Gospel Model. In the Bible, the Epistle to Hebrews, chapter 11, starting with verse one, is the beginning of the explanation from God about His model of child rearing and successful human behavior. This model is opposed to humanism in all its forms. An important listing of successful children and parents is presented here, along with the qualities that were passed down from fathers to sons, which made this list unique. Paul catalogs the experiences of those he knew who followed the Gospel Model. All these successfully used the Gospel Model and rejected humanism with all its subtlety.

Enoch walked with God and had a testimony that he pleased God. Enoch somehow grew up and survived the same harsh world that destroyed Cain. Enoch was brought up in *the way*. This points out that if one wants to walk with God in His way, it can be done. Enoch fit the pattern or image God originally created for children. Noah, by following this same pattern, was able to save his children while the children of all others perished in the flood. Those who perished depended on their own ingenuity (humanism) to save them. Noah had an adaptable lifestyle.

Abraham, who began the biblical trilogy of Abraham, Isaac and Jacob as parent-to-son-to-parent, is perhaps the best example of a parent who found *the way* of an absolute God. His life is an example of *the way*. God has a path for us to follow. As you recall, the blessing to Abraham was a reinstatement of the blessing to Adam and Eve and Noah. God wants to re-instate the blessing in the face of His great enemy of humanism.

It is good to see the future for your children; you should visualize them to be successful people. Moses did not by accident turn aside to see the burning bush that contained the presence of God. His mother guided him as a baby down the Nile River into Pharaoh's palace. His real mother was hired to nurse him and she brought Moses up to know the Hebrew God. Samuel did not by chance hear the voice of God speak to him out of the night. Samuel's mother brought him to the house of God and into the service of the Lord as a small child. Parents have all the tools necessary in the Gospel Model to raise their children. It is best to prepare and structure these tools in a manual for the future. It will remind you to build in them a proper heart like Moses, Samuel, and David possessed.

At the right time in life they will find their way by this structured *way* of thinking and responding. With this proper heart they will hear the voice of God and see the burning bush, they will do great and mighty acts. This is how to raise children the Bible way. God gave us Christ as a model and the means to enable us to make the best use of Christ.

Keep and use the information about the experiences that you and your family have had with God. Speaking often about these experiences will make God more real in the eyes of children. The family of Abraham, Isaac, and Jacob is the greatest family in the world. Every time in the Old Testament these three family names are mentioned, great promises to their children are revisited. There is a steady flow of blessings running through the family of God. In the book of Exodus 32:13, when Moses prayed to God to deliver Israel from Egypt, he asked God to remember Abraham, Isaac, and Israel (Jacob). These were great servants to whom God promised to make their family as numerous as the stars of heaven and the sand of the seashores. God replied to Moses with this answer: *I give unto your seed, and they shall inherit it for ever.*

In Deuteronomy 9:5 God promised to drive out the enemies of the children of this trilogy of Abraham, Isaac, and Jacob. Within the family unit God makes this promise to parents today to drive out the enemies of developing children. 2 Kings 13:23 tells how the LORD was gracious, had compassion, and had respect for this family unit and its children. If parents have children who have gone out of the way, 2 Chronicles 30:6, God promises to bring them back into the way. How God deals with our children demonstrates the kind of respect God has for people who follow Him, praise Him, and tell of His wonderful doings.

Inside a godly family is information that can save this drug-infected generation that is at risk. At least, if others do not wish to claim God's promise, there is information that can save your children. The Bible provides the understandings of *how* to raise children, *how* to make them successful, and *how* to be well adjusted. People who believe in God need to turn to God first for advice and information about child rearing.

The Hebrew people have been notorious for keeping genealogies that traced their heritage back to Abraham. This was their way of strongly keeping the faith within the family. By a powerful faith Abraham is exercising control over his descendents today. Note this in your handbook: God puts you in control forever when you follow God's *way*. Proverbs 22:6 assumes parents will know *the way* children should be raised. God expects believers to study the Gospel Model to gain information on how to raise children within the family.

Life is confusing without a pattern to follow. That is why we have road maps, anatomy charts, blueprints, scientific models and, the Gospel Model for raising children. Bible study using the Gospel Model creates confidence in how to pick and choose the information that is safe to use with your children. Parents will learn how to put information together that really works with children. It can be as easy as reading a road map.

Parents Store Up Knowledge

But his mother kept all these sayings in her heart. (Luke 2:51)

The above verse is a positive message for those who store up knowledge. Parents who have the correct knowledge are placed in control of the factors that determine whether or not children will be successful in school, on the playground, and in adult life. Knowledge really is power. When parents learn to use the Bible like a handbook and manual, when parents can make meaningful notations about life and their children, they gain and possess the cognitive skills to think like Christ. Taking notes is laying up spiritual wealth to be used in a time of need. The many things I learned from the Quick Success children would have been overlooked had their case studies not been on paper.

You alone, if need be, can best save your children from failure as you learn to immunize and protect children against the effects of destructive life events. You no longer need to depend on the teacher, principal, or minister for workable solutions. Know for yourself that you have the answer for the needs of children.

Do you have personality problems, worries, depressive episodes, and conflicts for which you are seeking a solution? A wonderful side effect of parents noting how to assist children in personality development is that it is virtually impossible to improve children's psychology without correcting your own flaws. This is the way God works. By helping others, you receive the greatest benefit. It is like the man who pulled the spike out of his own eye so he could see clearly to pull spikes out of the eyes of others. (Matthew 7:3)

The Gospel Model reveals clearly mistakes of child rearing before the mistakes breed SINS. The cliché is true: prevention is the best cure. By working with and learning the model you see mistakes you and others have been making in child rearing and wonder why you did not see these previously. Most people are amazed at their long ignorance of the facts, especially while the solutions to their problems were so obvious and simple. It is easier to say to yourself, "I told you so" than to have a school official or policeman to tell you what parental mistakes you have made. You can be in control.

All human behavior is learned. Behavior can be taught and behavior that leads to success can be taught. Use the following fact as an ally to take control of your children. Parents have more influence on the beliefs of children than any other persons do. Children naturally want to please their parents above all others. Since the trend today is to abdicate parental responsibility, it has become acceptable to believe that teachers, principals, and ministers have more influence on children than parents do. In fact, a former first lady wrote a book, which declared by its title, that it takes a whole village to raise a child. Community support does help, but you can by yourself, if need be, instill into your children everything they need to learn in order to be successful in life. You are the expert even if you do not know it. You must not surrender any parental authority.

Do not become discouraged. Children can be protected or immunized from the effects of adverse life events by parents. Children cannot be sheltered from the death of grandparents, a pet, a friend, or the lack of status and wealth. But every child, especially your child, can be protected against the bad effects of adverse life events. You can build in children a personality that stands up to adversity and leads to success in life. This learned lifestyle is called GOALS and it does place parents and children in control.

On the other hand, there is a personality that crumbles in the face of adversity, which leads to failure, depression, oppositional attitudes, defiant disorders, and learning gaps and delays. This learned lifestyle is called SINS. One personality comes from God and the other from faulty child rearing. The Gospel Model will identify the personality type you are teaching.

Parents can begin a new initiative after learning the Gospel Model. Ask the teachers and principals what they are doing to establish an identifiable plan of action for children at risk. Schools have all types of tests to evaluate academic performance. But, few tests are used to determine the emotional level of students, such as *Beck's Depression Inventory for Children*. Somebody in every school should be in charge of identifying students that are at risk to develop sad feelings and responses. As a Christian you may be able to participate in saving a number of children from a life of failure by asking the correct question at the right time. This is the greatest honor Christian parents can have, saving a child. We hope you are excited about beginning this search and creating a working hand-book and manual about the Gospel Model.

CHAPTER FIFTEEN

Preparing the Church "to Be" an Action-Doing Verb

Goal Oriented Preparation

Like a new car that comes off the assembly line, before it can be sold to the public, it must be given special care. The transmission, motor, and all moving parts must be given lubrication fluids. Even then, it will take some driving and time for the automobile to give up its stiffness and gain a more flexible mobility. You are preparing a plan to use the Gospel Model. You are not perfect but you are part of a perfect body. You cannot be perfect alone, just like a door of an automobile is not a perfect door until attached to the body of the car. Being a part of an active and assertive church will give you reason to work as a part of the body (Ephesians 5:27).

The first step to prepare the church to be a *Christian Assertive Effort* church is to act at moving the gospel into society. All parts must work towards the Great Commission. The church is never the church unless it acts to achieve its goals. To intellectually accept the primary goal, but at the same time not to be willing to do the things necessary to accomplish the goal, is a rejection of the Lord Jesus Christ.

God defined Himself as a verb when He said, "I AM" (Exodus 3:14). To be the church is to do the church thing just like God is God because He does the God thing. The church, to be the church, must address itself to the needs of the community it serves. If you do not sense that God is doing something in your community, He probably is not. If you are not doing something for God, you are not part of the church.

To follow the Gospel Model, one must be a doer of the Word. Pastor John Doe had an assertive church that recognized the stresses and dangers with which parents had to contend. Parents needed to be trained to be strong in the faith in order to ward off dangerous situations for children. There was a committee to teach parents what the Bible said about child rearing and the Gospel Model. Pastor John Doe had convinced the church that their religious beliefs worked and they were using their beliefs. This church had classes for young parents to teach them how to use the Gospel Model to raise children. The church was "being" by doing. To understand this is to understand the Gospel Model of Christ.

There was an effort in John Doe's church to minister to parents who had children at risk. Pastor John Doe had a growing church. People who did not normally attend church were coming to special meetings to receive training. Professionals, like teachers and lawyers as well as homemakers, wanted to use the Gospel Model in their work. Special attention was given to providing a Christian education to children in the public schools— a taboo of humanism. His church offered in-service training to parents and teachers on how to use the Gospel Model.

In a dying church the most often quote is "Nobody wants to do anything" or "You cannot get anybody to help." The term *dying church* does not exactly express what happens to a church when its members refuse to do God's bidding. More scriptural might be the term *perishing (disappearing)* for that is what inactive churches are doing. By doing spiritual things, one creates the church. By not doing, the church simply fails to be. For not following the commands of God, Christ says in the book of the Revelation of Christ, chapter two, that Christ simply removes the candlestick from inactive churches. Individual church members by their actions can make the church live and give light to others. If this fails and the church is not doing, my advice is for you to get out before the church disappears and you with it.

In the New Testament, the book of Acts is properly named. Acts demonstrates how God wants the church to be organized, prepared for growth, and ready to act. If the actions of the early church had not been well planned through the Gospel Model, Christianity would have died or perished. Christ—the real model—came to visit the disciples (Acts 1:3). It was from gathering together with Christ that the early Christians knew how to "possess one's vessel" (1 Thessalonians 4:4). Making use of the Holy Spirit was new to them. With the Holy Spirit, they too could speak the Word as the Spirit gave them utterance. The reason the hearers were able to understand what the Spirit was saying was that Jesus had already structured their hearts to receive the living Word. The miracle was not the speaking of the Word but in the actual hearing or receiving of the Word. Everybody whose heart was prepared heard the Word. I believe that a society that has not had its heart prepared by the church will not hear the Word as well as a society that has had its heart prepared.

It was vital that the early church members were sincere about their commitment and dedication to the Great Commission, as Ananias and Sapphira found out in Acts 5. It is true, one must go to church for the right reasons. Being untruthful cost them their lives. Their deaths were a real warning to the church that the behavior of the church had to be different than that of society. Feigned dedication is not a part of the Gospel Model (1 Peter 1:22). People are still dying both physically and spiritually because they would rather fake religion than live it.

Peter, John, and. James established the church with "committees" similar to what we have in churches today. Gifts and tithes were collected and accounted for by a special accounting committee (Acts 4:32). Some gave all they had, but persons were provided for according to their needs. They were focused on what they were to do.

The first church at Jerusalem numbered in the thousands. It took a very active committee to distribute to all their needs. There was a special committee for providing to needs of widows, orphans, and the poor. Stephen was chairman of this committee, but this did not exclude him from the number one goal and responsibility of preaching the Word. Stephen died being stoned for preaching Jesus Christ. Faithful in all things including menial chores, keeping his eyes on Christ whom he saw on the right hand of the Father in heaven, by his actions he provided this testimony: *And Stephen, full of faith and power, did great wonders and miracles among the people* (Acts 6:8).

Stephen's miracles were performed by his doing for the helpless and needy. He was always "doing" the Christian thing among his people, the members of the church. Stephen did not do a lot of healing, raising the dead, or restoring of sight, but he cleaned a lot of tables. To the hungry and poor, no doubt, the miracles and wonders that Stephen worked were providing for children, widows, and otherwise helpless persons who could not fend for themselves.

Not a lot is said about helpers like Stephen but the Bible held this category of Christians in high regard, referring to helpers as the messengers of the church (2 Corinthians 8:23). Stephen was "doing" the church thing among the people of the church. The vision is clear. People, who come to church to worship, need to see themselves as helpers for the purpose of doing miracles and wonders.

Rev. Doe's church had a committee that attended PTA meetings, school board hearings, and meetings of government and civic policy making agencies for the purpose to represent the community's point of view of an absolute God. These groups graciously defined the value system the local community wanted to follow. They requested that each agency announce and explain the basis on which decisions were made, especially the decisions that affected children. Christian citizens make up the majority of most public agencies, which are surprised to discover that they are following humanism. Talking to these fellow Christians will expose and uncloak humanism. If your church saves or protects just one child from failure, if one parent gives your church credit for making their child successful, your church will grow into what Pastor John Doe's church was. His church was really involved in community dialogue.

Growth becomes self-perpetuating in a Gospel Model church. Sow the seed on fertile ground and it will produce a hundred fold. As growth begins, people will come forward to ask, "What can I do?" And the beat goes on: as one church in a community has success with the Gospel Model, a church in the next community follows.

An Action-designed Plan

When God told Moses "I AM," He could only refer to Himself for there was nothing else great enough to which He could be compared. The fact that God defined Himself as a verb is significant to the fact that He was whatever He was doing. To Moses and the children of Israel, God was the redeemer, because He redeemed them. To be redeemed the Hebrews needed only to follow God's image as He led them out of Egypt. To those who rebelled, the Lord was the God of anger (Genesis 18:30).

Man is made in God's image so much that we too are "whatever we are doing" at any given time. Jesus said that we are servants to whomever we give ourselves to follow. There can be only one master. If we do righteousness, we have God as our master. If we do evil, we have Satan as our master. GOALS—*God's Oriented Adaptive Life Style*—is one choice. SINS—*Satan's Inadequate Naturalistic Style*—is another choice. Jesus said that we could not follow Him unless we chose GOALS. What Jesus was saying is that we could not choose both lifestyles. The choice is either the Lord or the devil. To use the words of Jesus, to attempt to choose both would result in being spit out of the kingdom of God (Revelation 3:16). People spit when they have something nasty or offensive in their mouth. A non-working Christian fits this description well in the eyes of God.

The difficulty is to understand the Gospel Model well enough to be able to follow Christ as the model. Use this book as a manual of the Gospel Model until the model begins teaching you from its own power. The purpose of this book is to teach Christians to make the explanation of the Gospel Model practical in use in society. Christians are expected to do everything by the example of Jesus Christ (Romans 14:8). Just as children learn to talk by talking, to walk by walking, and to read by reading, Christians learn to use the Gospel Model by using Jesus Christ (Isaiah 9:6).

In the name of God is found the totality of the meaning of life. Christ counsels, solves conflicts, builds houses (hearts), directs paths, protects, immunizes (from SINS), and provides mental and physical health. Christians bring these qualities to society and pass the blessing, which is the ability to raise children, from one generation to the next. Study the dynamics of the model to use it in all walks of life. Use it in conferences, counseling, orientation of committees, education, politics, professional focus, and in all things. God expects you to use the Gospel Model 100% in everything you do.

Age of Accountability

The Gospel Model teaches that parents are to train and prepare children for that day, the day children become accountable for their own moral behavior. Too many Christian parents do not prepare children for this day. The actions of parents are always training children towards the age of accountability when children can choose for themselves the family religion. Training is an important part of teaching. Training is used with children before they are able to understand correct behavior. For example, a four or five-year old has no idea what it is to be sexually immoral. But parents train a child to be modest and to respect the anatomy of his or her body.

Jesus said that both good (training) and evil (training) come from the heart. Parents are the major builders of the heart in children, just like a carpenter builds a house. Ideally, Christian parents use the Gospel Model to prepare the hearts of children to accept God. That is what Moses' mother did for Moses. The building of GOALS will have laid out the way for children to go.

Some parents inadvertently have allowed SINS to become the lifestyle of children, which makes it difficult to choose God's way of living when the age of accountability arrives. As children come of age, begin to think more about why they respond to stimuli, and become more analytical about responses, it is at this point where the Gospel Model must be used to influence what children will continue to believe to be true. Children do evaluate the past actions of parents. Many times adults express joy and sadness over the way parents raised them.

In adolescent and early adulthood development, children become more intellectually inquisitive about what they believe. They have been conditioned to believe in God and Christian values, if they are from Christian homes. As they question their acceptance of faith, it is important that the answers be provided on the spot to the intellectual soundness of what they have been trained to accept. Adolescents often question why we believe in God, why we go to church, why we believe in heaven and hell, why do we go to school, why do we not fight, steal, and murder? If they have been trained to respond in the correct manner, they will accept God when it comes time for them to choose from their hearts and minds.

Since not all children come from Christian homes, it is at this point, the point when children ask what is right and wrong, that Christian evangelism can provide intervention to a child who has learned a maladaptive lifestyle or SINS. Christian schoolteachers might be the only lights God has available to light up children's lives. That is why Christians can never allow the lamp to burn low.

Both children with GOALS and SINS, each having a lifestyle they have learned, will have an opportunity to choose which way to go in life. Good persons more often than not chose to continue in a lifestyle of GOALS, whereas the SINS lifestyle is more difficult to give up; but there were many thieves, killers, and liars who promised Christ that they would kill and steal no more. Many who have lived riotous lives have reformed. Yet, Jesus pointed out the fact that the path leading to destruction was well worn. Keep your light shining for these children following in SINS. Your light may save them.

Christians call this choosing the coming to the age *of accountability*. The choosing of a lifestyle is being *born again*. Will the adolescent choose to keep his Christian values? This is a question Satan tries to answer by using every possible method of doubt to interfere with the reasoning process. God does ask His children to come to reason with Him. Satan wants children and adults to have a confused mind as much as possible when going to God to reason with God. Satan seeks to make it difficult for the

Word to penetrate the heart especially at the time of accountability.

Intellectual Preparation of the Church

When children come to the age of accountability, they need to be prepared intellectually, that is, they need to have already been trained to accept Christ. The Gospel Model prepares children for an intellectual development and provides an answer *for the reason of the hope that is in his heart"* (1 Peter 3:15). Parents should be using the Gospel Model in working towards creating a child-person who is capable of discovering God as a personal experience at a specific time of accountability. It is a long-time belief of Christians that children come to the age of maturity when they too can choose to follow God.

Situations occur that will make young people question the validity of their faith. We all have knowledge of persons who claimed to follow Christ, but have behaved in ways that belie their being a Christian. The Bible teaches that there is a lifestyle that can be defended intellectually and backed up by living. That is the way we convince the world of Jesus Christ. Nobody expects parents to be perfect, but to give a perfect testimony to children about a perfect God, all one has to do is be willing to repent and confess the mistakes made. Children will recognize that the behavior of adults, while not perfect, is righteous simply because the adults disapprove of their own bad behavior. Although Christians may not always live up to a high standard of perfection, they do not lower the standard. Just keep trying! That is how to give a perfect testimony of Jesus Christ.

The image of Christ is what God expects us to copy. What modern religion has done, however, is to choose the characteristics of man, which are the easiest to copy rather than the more difficult ones of a high standard and image of a perfect absolute God. For example, it is easy to make the church financially solvent by giving tithes and offerings, an important part of worship. But Jesus points out that this type of giving was not one of the more valuable parts of worship. You can do several additional, more important acts of worship and not have any money to give. These acts were things done with our minds and hearts (Matthew 23:23).

Preparation for a Philosophical World System

Christians are presenting to society a worldview that says how things really should be. The Gospel Model rivals and over-shadows any of the great world philosophic and religious systems. Satan has many philosophic systems with which to confuse mankind. God has only one and He makes His worldview clear in the model of Christ (2 Corinthians 3:2).

Satan's viewpoint is humanism. An example of just one humanistic worldview is called *determinism*. Determinists sometimes use the model of the atom to explain what the universe is like. In a deterministic model, the *cause* of the first atom to move was God. From the time the first atom moved, all other happenings in the universe were determined forever from the first atom that moved. The god in determinism does not recognize free will or choice. He does not even recognize himself. After the first movement, he is no longer needed. This god is unable to intervene in history. No requirement exists that a god be involved in the universe after the *first cause*. Everything has already been determined. The first movement of the first atom in the universe has determined one's fate and the fate of the universe.

Needless to say, this is not the model of the universe that Christians believe to be real. But in Christ's day, the Stoics and Epicureans, spoken of in the Book of Acts, were *determinists*, believing in *fate* and whatever was to be will be. Today the true Stoics also believe that whatever will be will be. The Gospel Model is the model early Christians used to defeat the arguments of the Stoics and

Epicureans. The major difference was that the philosophy of Jesus Christ provided a living, caring ontological God who granted man free will. The Christian God intervenes in history to change things, whereas the god of determinism is not involved with mankind, as history is already determined. Man is on his own.

The Gospel Model best explains interventions of God into human affairs. The Gospel Model mentally connects the physical with the spiritual. It explains the meaning of existence. The Gospel Model's metaphysical and rational basis is used to instruct Christians how to do counseling, conflict management, ethics, educational theorizing, and Christian philosophy. The Gospel Model is designed by God to show us how to live with a purpose and in harmony with the universe. God does this with His perfect Gospel Model of Christ.

Use the Philosophy of Jesus Christ

Jesus Christ taught well the five branches of philosophy. *Metaphysics* (what is real), *epistemology* (how do we know), *logic* (correct inferences), *ethics* (how man should live) and *science* (how things work) are the five branches of philosophy. To Jesus there was only one true philosophy or doctrine, and it alone explained all the categories of philosophical thought.

> *Jesus answered them, and said, My doctrine is not mine, but his that sent me. If any man will do his will, he shall know of the doctrine, whether it be of God, or whether I speak of myself.* (John 7:16–17)

The gospel truth is so simple and clear that the only chance Satan has is to confuse mankind by multiplying lies into many philosophies. The proliferation of philosophies tends to confuse Christians in the thinking process. Jesus pointed out that men taught *for doctrines the commandments of men* and that their attempts to worship God was vanity (Mark 7:7).

Christ did not object to persons knowing philosophies other than His. We are to consider the ways of Satan. Christ does, however, want us to know our own Christian philosophy well enough to answer the questions of men and Satan. By understanding the truth, you make yourself free to see the errors others have fallen into by their incorrect thinking of humanism. Christ compared correct thinking to building a house on a rock. Christians need to compare their thoughts and beliefs to the Gospel Model to evaluate their true soundness and usefulness.

God is preparing us to live everlasting life in the spiritual world, a world of action. But clearly God wants us to practice living the spiritual life here as preparation for the after life. Jesus taught that how we live in the temporal society determines what our rewards and status in the spiritual society will be.

God used the model of Christ in creating the universe. The Gospel Model was present in creation for a purpose. The Bible says that *from the beginning He choice us to salvation* (2 Thessalonians 2:13). This was the goal and purpose of God in creation. Bringing salvation through Christ is God's main goal. Christ is what *He is doing*. He fulfilled His purpose in sending the Son to save all men (2 Thessalonians 2:13). Christ became a savior by saving us.

God was the creator of all things. God created moral law. Humanistic relativity is not permitted. The freedom to choose is that one can choose between God's absolute law or Satan's many doctrines. God demanded man to be a philosophical creature, basing decision on thinking like Christ thought. Paul said to allow the mind of Christ to be in us. Behaving like Christ or living a spiritual life are one and the same.

The church operates outside the Gospel Model when it speaks in platitudes and euphemisms, rather than being willing to act out the real truth. God's truth must not be set aside through euphemistic language. This is a scheme of SINS to convince Christians that they are not responsible to live by what they believe. To use a euphemistic definition of honesty like "that's business" instead of "you shall not steal" is to apply relativity to its meaning, thereby changing the commandment. Using deceit in business should be a clue that one does not really believe it is evil to steal and really does not believe in a God that requires accountability. God moves into man's understanding of things with truths not seen. Men must act in harmony with God to possess all God wants man to have.

To Jesus, evil was Satan. Evil did not use loud horns and drums to put the church to sleep. He praises the church for being politically correct and for acquiescing to a more moderate and liberal philosophy of religion, a more euphemistic faith. Anybody can live by a faith that allows one to cheat, lie, steal, and murder. Otherwise, Satan leaves the church alone to allow it to die on its own.

Man is not Enough

Faith in God is at odds with the belief that man can save himself. In the New Testament the theme of the book of Revelation of Jesus Christ reveals God's way of doing battle with evil. Jesus Christ is pictured as a great warrior defending against evil with the Word of God coming out of Jesus' mouth as a devouring sword. The true conflict in the world really is a battle of words. That is why God chose preaching as the way to save the world (1 Corinthians 1:21). God uses the model of Jesus Christ to destroy His enemies and establish the Word.

Humanism, a euphemistic belief, has a different point of view. The source of knowledge for a humanist is man himself. Man is the source of all truth. The humanist would say that there is no higher authority in the universe than man. If there is a God, they say, we cannot know Him. Humanistic religious beliefs rule out the belief in an ethical and absolute law as a voice of authority. A person who claims to be an existentialist begins his explanation of the universe with his own existence. Nothing else is needed but his existence. This is an example of a very weak humanist point of view. To a Christian everything begins with a need for God.

The Nazis derived their authority to extinguish the Jews with the excuse that they were attempting to improve the human race. They looked at themselves as being noble and with the courage to do what needed to be done. In fact, it was their duty to improve the race of mankind by killing the weak so as to create the *super-man*.

A new acceptance of humanism by society demonstrates that society is beginning to believe that the worst of humanism is in the past. After World War II, subtly and gradually the American culture has been willing to adopt humanism for public schools, political debates; all this, with the rejection of an absolute God in public life. Man is attempting to subtly place himself back on the moral throne. Is man claiming that he has improved himself that much to once again to compete with God as the voice of authority? This is a theory of knowledge that Christians must reject.

Humanism is the basis of logic for most liberal points of view. Man has the right to choose what is morally correct. This is the reasoning behind the abortionist and the theory of moral relativity. Christ's Gospel Model is not a model of relativity. The right to have an abortion is a humanistic belief stating that man can choose when to kill. Many Christians agree with the abortionist's point of view but this is a point of view that comes from a humanistic model. It is the same logic used in the killing of six million Jews. There is a difference between a woman having an abortion and the Nazis killing Jews, but the authority and logic to do so are the same.

Satan is subtle. He slips into society a few beliefs that seem practical. Some of the tenets of humanism are practical but the practicality is simply bait to catch bigger fish. Humanism says that everybody must exclude God to protect the rights of a single humanist or atheist. Pushing this point of view forward has led to the abandonment of prayer in public schools, the rejection of the Ten Commandments in courtrooms and schools, and glorified the right to choose a sexual lifestyle.

The subtlety of humanism is so prominent in our culture that to attack the views of humanism is politically incorrect. It is time to say something about American values. Note that that the Christian philosophical battle is against humanism. Jesus accused the Pharisees and scribes of following a humanistic model but they denied this. Hypocrites of Jesus' day accepted humanism but they did not know it. They were pleasers of men being politically correct. It will take a great philosophical effort to rid the Judeo-Christian culture of humanism. It will at least require that Christians learn and use the Gospel Model properly.

How did Jesus reveal to men that they followed humanism? Jesus spent much of His time forcing adults to examine, weigh, and think about their actions. Jesus asked the correct questions to force correct choices from all those who were recorded in His book of life (Acts 2:47). He drew words in the sand that reminded the Pharisees of how God would want them to treat people who sinned. It was the evil in their hearts that sought to kill the woman who had committed adultery. Children learn to throw stones when they see adults throwing stones.

The Pharisees wanted to stone the woman caught in the act of adultery but being reminded of their own sins, they were powerless to harm her. The Pharisees, who faced their own sins, became followers of Christ. Those who could not face their sins, did not. Christ forced them to examine themselves by comparing their behavior with the behavior of what Jesus would do (John 8:7).

Jesus always forces men to examine their behavior. The significance of this examination is that Christ does not want adults to pass their bad behavior on to children. Jesus pointed out that a person who taught others to do evil by what they did would be in spiritual trouble, whereas those who taught men to do good by their actions would be in line for spiritual reward (Matthew 5:19).

A significant number of times Jesus began the examination process by asking a question. To Peter, Jesus asked, *Who do men say that I am* and followed the question with another of *Who do you say that I am*. What was expected of Peter? After the resurrection of Jesus, Peter was expected to teach and strengthen the brethren (Luke 22:32). Religious leaders were men of power and Jesus was daily in the synagogues asking and answering questions of them. We are told that Jesus began the questioning and answering process when He was twelve years old (Luke 2:42).

Jesus asked rhetorical questions, not to win an intellectual debate or to prove a point, but to unlock the door of the heart to allow the power of God to flow through. Like Jesus, Christians must move beyond the defense of individual points of few. Jesus asked questions as a prerequisite for spiritual light to enter the heart. Christ forced the Pharisees to do self-examination. It will surprise you what you learn as you construct questions for others and for yourself. Remember the parable of the rich man. He spoke to his heart but failed to ask the question of who would inherit his possessions after his death. Had he only asked the question, the epiphany of God's message could have flowed through to his heart.

The use of questions to answer questions is called the *Socratic method*, and is noted for creating intellectual agony in others. Asking questions cost Socrates his life. Jesus asked soul-searching questions and demonstrated great skill in this method. He was crucified. Socrates was poisoned. But you will be liberated from humanism and the strongholds of Satan if you seek the truth through a godly question. Jesus used the questioning method to save souls. God searches hearts and He uses the condemnation of the Holy Spirit to illuminate what is in hearts. Jesus asked questions to lead people to truth.

An example of the proper use of a question today would be for a group of Christians appearing before a school board to ask that the educational philosophy of the school system be explained. By asking the correct questions, it is possible to inform board members and politicians of the philosophical basis upon which they are actually operating. People sometimes discover they are following humanism when their true intentions are to follow Christ. Once seeing how they actually respond, once the basis of behavior is examined, people willingly change to a style of behavior they think is most appropriate. When discovering what righteousness really meant, the Pharisees left alone the woman caught in adultery. Most school board members probably believe in Jesus Christ. Throwing stones is most likely not what they want to do.

Whereas most public officials operate from a humanistic point of view, which is a religious point of view, they actually believe in and personally support the Christian model of behavior. People in such agencies are not aware that they function under a philosophical standard of which they themselves disapprove.

Two life styles are illuminated in response to a Gospel Model question, GOALS or SINS. Once school boards understand that their policies are not following absolute law, but humanism, education in your community will improve. Humble yourself when asking questions, for a good question will disturb the peace (Matthew 10:34). Jesus was chased out of towns, synagogues, and communities by the humanists for asking so many questions. People did not like it. Those who thought of themselves as righteous learned to hate and despise Jesus. Asking the right question can be a ruthless act. It is best to have a goodly number of citizens together to ask questions to soften the blow.

A public leader may not appreciate being told that he follows an evil philosophy. The evil philosophies, having originated from human beings, are grouped under a broad classification of *humanism*. Humanism is the antichrist as referenced by 1 John 2–4. You can imagine the type of response gathered from a public figurer being cast in the role of an antichrist.

The Three-step Method

Developing the art of asking a question about what one wants to accomplish is vital in making the Gospel Model dynamic. Start with a stated goal. I want to be a doctor. I want to earn money. I want good health. I want to be a godly person. These are all stated goals. Stating goals is the first step in making the Gospel Model a dynamic force. Secondly, by asking either yourself or others questions what must be done to accomplish a goal, one quickly finds out what action to take. Goals can be as comprehensive as to cover a lifetime of living such as a goal to be a minister or doctor or as simple as wanting to scratch the itch on your back. The secret is to go after what you want. The action that must be taken could last a lifetime or a few seconds.

After identifying a goal and determining what actions must occur for the attainment of the goal, start the effort to be a goal achiever. State the goal: I want to win the fifty-yard dash. That is the target. Ask the question: What must I do to win the race? You must enter the race. You must train. You must discipline yourself. In step one, you are a person who wants to win a race. The outcome is being a winning racer via the actions done, by training and discipline. You are at step three and also back to step one. Step one leads logically to step two: I want to be a two time champion runner.

Look at the goal, which will suggest a pattern of behavior that must exist, then, determine how the model for accomplishing the goal unfolds. This simple but effective method becomes the most valuable tool of all when doing conferencing, counseling, and conflict management. The three-step approach becomes a dynamic, action model of doing. You are what you do. You do what needs to be done to achieve goals, which creates what you are. You are a runner, a doctor, a nurse, and you are what you do. The formula is Goal equals Question times Effort = Success = Being (who I am).

Learning to operate the three-step method will assist you in helping yourself and others at building and rebuilding personalities one goal at a time. By using the three-step approach, a habit of saintly behavior will develop in your life as every time you assist others, you improve yourself.

Understand what you are doing with this effort. You are constantly building the kingdom of God. Again, note that the kingdom is within you (Luke 17:21). All the efforts made contribute to building your heart and the heart of others. Every person who has built something knows it is easier to begin with a plan in mind. In home construction, rebuilding often has to be done to correct mistakes in the structure because the plans were not completely followed. Sometimes rebuilding requires radical measures. A carpenter can consult with the model or blueprints to tell which adjustments are necessary.

Keep the Gospel Model dynamic by using the three-step method. With children this is the type of intervention that is necessary. If something goes wrong, go back to the model. Better yet, in personality development, doing it right the first time is best and means major reconstruction does not take place as often. Following the model and not having to go back to do it again, is called *prevention*, which is better than a cure or intervention. But, if it is not correct and you want to go back, you can. You can, if you know where all the parts are and how to put them in proper order. Knowing the model of what you want built is important.

Paul said in Romans 12:1–2 that parents were to rebuild and renew their minds by the Gospel Model and not to do things the way humanistic society does things. Paul says to build according to the Gospel Model, which indicates a Christian is to develop new and unique mindsets, different than the mindsets that non-Christians have. Adults who convert to Christ have to rebuild. This is Christ's intervention. With renewed mindsets, new Christians make the automatic responses to life events that God the Father wants them to make.

Can you see the three-step method in the question *what must I do to be saved* (Acts 16:30)? Again, people want eternal life from Jesus. That was their stated goal. Next, the question was asked: *what must I do* (Matthew 19:16)? I believe that one way or another, everybody that is saved has asked this question.

In the epistle to the Philippians (4:8), Paul encouraged the church to think from the heart on good things. A loving, wonderful question facilitates thinking on good things and finding great solutions to the human dilemma that Satan has attempted to completely confuse.

> *Finally, brethren, whatsoever things are true, whatsoever things are honest, whatsoever things are just, whatsoever things are pure, whatsoever things are lovely, whatsoever things are of good report; if there be any virtue, and if there be any praise, think on these things.*

The analogy is that parents need to provide good thoughts, as building material that will train children in the lifestyle that automatically makes them successful and saintly. Being successful in life can be an automatic response coming from a child's heart. In this way children are transformed into what parents want them to become. Peter refers to this scenario as "living stones" built up as a "spiritual house" and accepted by God (1 Peter 2:5).

A careful observer can see what individuals think in their hearts. When a child wants to join in a game but senses that other children do not want him, this sense tells him that he is not worthy or good enough. Especially parents can see this. Who is the child who thinks he is not worthy? He does not play games with other children. He stands by and watches with a mindset of low self-esteem. You might say his heart is not in it. He is the one who does not have an expectation to be accepted, but hopes playtime will end. A careful observer can see these things. Children and adults are the same.

They think things and feel thoughts but cannot explain why they feel the way they do. They are what they think, which is the reason that in clubs, PTA's, sports and churches that more people stand on the sidelines than participate. Children who do not participate are showing the signs leading to sick emotional health from bad mindsets in the heart. Christians and churches that do not participate in activities of the kingdom are spiritually ill. This can all change, if churches and parents are willing to rebuild with the Gospel Model as their guide. Churches must be active: no activity, no church.

State a goal. Determine what needs to be done to establish the goal. Begin doing that thing that must be done. You become what you do just like Christ became the God of salvation by paying the penalty for sins. This is what He had to do. Jesus Christ said in John 13:34, *A new commandment I give unto you, That ye love one another; as I have loved you, that ye also love one another.*

The commandment was new, representing new information of how God expects us to live. Keeping the laws of Moses is simply not enough. When Jesus said to go into the highways and by-ways, the meaning was that Christians were to go out of the comfort zone to bring people into the kingdom (Luke 14:23). It will take some action to be the church. It takes action to be a Christian.

After the goal has been established, what must be done is rather obvious. An acquaintance of mine was not very popular with a group of men with which he played golf. They did not like the way he treated them, as it was his nature to tease them often. When they chose up to play golf in foursomes, he found himself left out although he was a better golfer than most of them. They did not view him as a nice fellow. After deciding it was too painful not to be liked, he established a goal to become better liked and accepted. He admitted that he was not well liked. He asked himself why he was not appreciated. Wasn't he a good golfer? He began to take notes of his behavior and listed the things he did that turned fellow golfers against him. After making a list of behaviors that he should not be doing, he began to change his ways. Little things that bothered him, he forced himself to ignore, like somebody talking on his shot or walking about while he was putting.

It was difficult at first. It took a whole year; but when he reevaluated who he was, he found out that people liked him after he made the changes in his behavior. He was being chosen to play in foursomes often. He felt like a worthy person. Who did he want to be? What must he do? Who has he become? That was following the Gospel Model in rebuilding personality. He was able to make a more meaningful witness to Christ and affected others differently. Becoming a nice fellow was planed. He did what had to be done. He became what He did. He learned from this experience that the Gospel Model works in every aspect of life. This experience led to other good experiences, all of which he noted in his handbook. It all began when he was willing to allow the old self to die and the new person to rise from the ashes. The sacrifice of the "self" improved the attitudes and spiritual well being of others as he created a person others could love.

Persons can improve personalities in children and themselves with three basic steps: know who you are, act and do, which makes you what your are, and set appropriate goals. These are the three simple steps of walking in the light of the Gospel Model. Internalize into your automatic response system these three steps in everything you do.

Prepare the Heart to be Your Guide

All the families in Quick Success were a little dysfunctional in their behavior. It was very easy to change the mindsets and the thinking of these children. But the parents' minds were also changed from failing parents to successful parents. We simply changed their mindsets and lifestyles, which came from their hearts, to those that produced success. When raising children in the Bible way, it can be very easy. The younger the children, the easier it is to influence mindsets. When our parents of Quick Success understood what they were to do for the children, they did it to themselves too. The method really worked well.

The heart is going to respond to life events automatically. Purifying the hearts of children is the secret to automatically building a healthy family unit and adult character.

This explains why David prayed for God to create in him a clean or pure heart after he had defiled his childlike heart (Psalm 51:5–10).

David needed the correct mindsets in specific areas of his thinking for automatically responding to truth and wisdom. It is good to be guided by the heart provided the heart is pure. Parents need to begin raising children to have pure hearts. To create a sound mind in David, God created a pure heart first. David was God's child and God makes his children into the image of His approval by beginning with the heart. This was firmly the belief of Jesus that children could be led to success in life with a pure heart. Look at the way God says people respond in life first from the heart.

A good man out of the good treasure of his heart bringeth forth that which is good; and an evil man out of the evil treasure of his heart bringeth forth that which is evil: for of the abundance of the heart his mouth speaketh, with the truth, the way, and life. (Luke 6:45)

Make a note to keep telling yourself to always work towards a pure heart. Children respond from their hearts first. When a child is old enough, he speaks; he develops an abundance of concepts that have trained him to automatically bring forth either good or evil. Whatever manner in which a child or adult responds, it is an indication of what the structure of the heart is like. To change the response one must change the heart. Better yet, parents need to build a good heart in their children that is pure. I like what Paul said in speaking to his children, that he was going to work with them until *Christ be formed in you* (Galatians 4:19).

Considering that Jesus said, *I am the way,* this is what parents need to work towards, forming *the way* in the hearts of children. To Christians at Rome, whom Paul thought of as his children, he said, *ye have obeyed from the heart that form of doctrine which was delivered you* (Romans 6:17). Model, form, structure, and the house were in their minds so they could obey God (Romans 12:2). You can train the heart.

My wife Sharon and I have used the Gospel Model with our son. My wife taught our son Josh that he was a handsome child. He thought well of himself. However, his playmates teased him because they said he was fat. His self-image was immediately threatened. We later taught him that beauty is as beauty does, a quality of beauty that he could control. Once he believed this, it was easier for him to be accepted by his friends and his self-image improved immediately. Josh's original mindset that he was a handsome child failed him because his concept of handsome was based entirely on appearance and not actions. His parents subtly intervened to change the way he thought. We still think Josh is handsome. Who knows what would have happened when he made a bad grade in school if we had previously taught him that he was smart? Would he then have thought he was dumb?

A child is targeted for failure when he does not learn to associate cause and effect with himself and what he does. Josh learned to respond to the mindset that he could change the world that teased him by using good behavior. Making friends was a short-term goal. As Josh has matured he is about to succeed at his adopted long-term goal of being a teacher and eventually a school principal. Like father, like son. When Josh graduated from high school he took one of the prettiest girls to the prom. She was the prom queen. He also is a good golfer.

One thing that I have learned through observing thousands of parents raising their children is that God never made a child that was not at risk to fail at something. Things happen. The best that parents can do is to prepare children with a personality that will resist the use of drugs, alcohol, immorality, and the acquisition of a negative attitude. Children themselves must learn to cast aside stumbling blocks so their way will lead to success in life. The fact is that the more intensely *the way* is instilled in the thought process of children's hearts and minds, the more immune they will be to at-risk factors. Note that you have just learned how to immunize children against failure and to add protection to their life.

Chapter Sixteen

Providing All God's Services

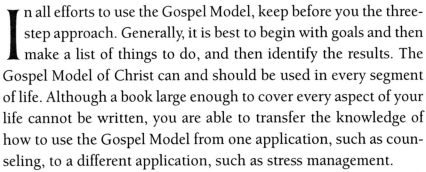

In all efforts to use the Gospel Model, keep before you the three-step approach. Generally, it is best to begin with goals and then make a list of things to do, and then identify the results. The Gospel Model of Christ can and should be used in every segment of life. Although a book large enough to cover every aspect of your life cannot be written, you are able to transfer the knowledge of how to use the Gospel Model from one application, such as counseling, to a different application, such as stress management.

There is a self-perpetuating teaching and learning factor built into the Gospel Model. Consistent with what Jesus taught in John, chapter 16, Christ is the truth and Christ promised the Holy Spirit would lead us to all truth (verse 13). Christians must put on the Gospel Model like putting on clothing. 2 Corinthians 5:4 reveals Christ is clothing to be put on. You can wear the Gospel Model.

Transfer knowledge to all necessary areas of Christian living. The Gospel Model fits perfectly the church's need to teach Christianity in public schools, conferencing, conflict management, managing stress, and addressing at-risk children. There is enough information in this book to get you well on the way to successfully raising children and using the Gospel Model.

You will also be influencing the opinion of society on how to raise children. It is important that churches buy into the Gospel Model approach. Jesus Christ works. He is the formula for success. *Raising Children the Bible Way* began by saying, "Religion can work for parents but it must be real religion; it must be something that people can trust."

My church is in decline in world membership. If I believe what has just been said, I must admit a few truths. First, Christ is not being used in my church like God has planed for us to use Him. It is not God's fault. As a church we are not doing the church thing. Believe me, we have tried many programs and approaches. We have even advertised on television and called aloud on radio. Nevertheless, the job is not getting done. From our own testimony we are not trusting God correctly. With our mouths and lips we are worshipping God, but our hearts are far from Him. We have not found the way to please God completely.

Secondly, pastors and teachers must admit they have not trusted God. They have leaned too heavily on their training and education and have failed to teach the church about Christ and how to trust Him. Thirdly, the church must admit it has not taught the anatomy of Christ very well. The end of decline begins with properly building the mind of Christ. This has not been done.

Pastors and teachers must ask the question of what must be done, lest we perish with denominational decline. Teach the church about the Gospel Model of Christ. We have called Him out as being God, but do we give Him credit for being what He is? When one explains the anatomy of God, all the parts add up to action. For the church to be part of Christ there must be action. Pastor Doe knew how to explain and to teach his people to follow a holy Verb. Once his people saw what needed to be done, they went to work. The goal was to be a lively stone, a growing church. They became that, through actions based on the Gospel Model.

Educational Theorizing and Curriculum Development

How can a teacher use the Gospel Model in teaching and avoid the dilemma of being politically incorrect in using the Gospel Model? What are the responsibilities of a Christian educator? These questions cannot be sidestepped but must be met head-on. These are questions waiting for an assertive effort to give the answers.

The Gospel Model can be used as a teaching model. No one questions the model used, unless the results of academic and social progress are less than required by a democratic government. The big word is *accountability*. What have you taught? What do the test scores say you have taught? Otherwise, teachers are free to use the Gospel Model as a basis for teaching.

The Gospel Model will not be attacked for the results it yields. Humanism is a political theory and it will resist the Gospel Model from a political basis. But Christian teachers must face accountability to God. Keep quiet, if you must, but be known by your works. Teach by the Gospel Model just like Mrs. Pal did in chapter one.

You can find authority for using the Gospel Model in American history. The Gospel Model philosophically adheres to the Constitution of the United States. For example, even though the Constitution clearly says, "All men are created equal" humanists do not want creationism taught in the public schools.

The Gospel Model derives its authority to be used in education from the belief in absolute Being. If society asks educators to teach morality, educators already have an absolute basis from which to teach morality that does not lapse into moral relativity or humanism. Humanistic educational philosophy opens the doors for drug abuse, sexual promiscuity, and even murder, all of which conflict with what local communities want. The problem with local schools is their inability to grasp the philosophical basis of the Constitution by which to say this behavior is acceptable and another is not. According to the Constitution moral relativity is not legal but saying what is right and wrong is. America is a Christian nation because most Americans practice Christianity. With the acceptance of this absolute standard of morality, teachers can teach moral behavior.

No generation of Americans has rejected absolute law. No president, vice president or court denies America is a nation of laws, although sometimes their decisions and actions refute this. Once we admit, however, that many boards and officers do actually believe in the Absolute, they will feel less compelled to serve humanistic causes and follow humanistic reasoning. Certainly, humanism will resist the Absolute. Courts will questions us. That is what we want. The question must be brought to the forefront of American law for review. The more we practice a constitutional way of living in our teaching, the more we will be heard and the more chances to change the thinking of the American people will be had.

Recall the chapter entitled "CHRISTIAN EDUCATION—IS IT ENOUGH?" To present a Christian education, one has only to use three basic steps, which we have called the three-step approach. The three-step approach should result in students learning GOALS and learning to be adaptable. It is this adaptability that children learn that gives them a Christian education.

School principals can teach the faculty to teach the Christian and constitutional model of behavior without reference to any particular religion. Teachers can use the three-step approach in developing a lesson plan. For example, if a teacher has a goal to teach several skills and attitudes to students, she simply lists the goals. The learning of reading and positive self-esteem are two very reachable goals. To achieve both goals, what must the teacher do? That is the question. Make sure to teach the reading facts on a level that students will be able to comprehend quickly. After building up self-confidence by getting quick answers, begin teaching the more difficult facts. Remind the students that they can learn the new facts because they learned the previous ones. As students learn the more difficult facts, they will think of themselves as being capable individuals.

In teaching a student, instruction is only part of the job. American schools are quick to point out that teachers must care for the whole child. A humanistic model cannot teach to the complete child because of that inherent moral relativity concept. A student's spirit, his moral character, and his future are responsibilities the teacher must address. An absolute model can only address these. One must know what is moral to teach morality. Make plans for using a Constitutional approach or a model of absolute law.

Conferencing Is Important

An attempt to deliberately use the Gospel Model in everything is important whether it is counseling children or adults. Keep the three-step approach in the forefront every time you speak, regardless of the forum. Ask, "What am I trying to say?" Teach parents the Gospel Model using the three-step approach, which makes conferencing and counseling easier and well targeted.

What you are attempting to say is your goal? Next, choose the words that will express what you are trying to say. The words chosen to begin expressing the goal are chosen with the goal in mind. For example, in conflict management how a word is said helps determine the word's meaning. Note that Proverbs 15:1 predicts that a softly spoken word turns wrath and anger aside. The type of response wanted from others greatly depends on the words used and how these are pronounced. In any conference, whether formal or informal, what and how the words are said makes a difference. Therefore, not only what is said is part of the goal attainment but also *how*. In conversations Christians especially need to weigh each word spoken so as not to leave the wrong impression. Christ only said it once but He meant it for all time: *But I say unto you, That every idle word that men shall speak, they shall give account thereof in the day of judgment* (Matthew 12:36).

It is difficult to get across the testimony of Jesus Christ, if you have a habit of speaking harshly. There can be a form of speaking a particular way, if you practice weighing your words to fit the occasion. For this reason James placed great emphasis on the tongue. The tongue sets the course of life on fire. It is the stern of a ship and difficult to control, especially in storms (James 3).

Jesus asked the disciples to conference the fullness of Christ in every activity in which they were engaged. Assert the complete Gospel of Jesus Christ to society. You cannot sanctify the Lord too much. Special benefits exist in the Gospel Model for Christian professionals who have made it their goal to live a sanctified life for God, especially for schoolteachers, guidance counselors, doctors, social workers, Christian lay persons, and ministers. There must be awareness that godly conferring best drives the message home (Romans 14:6).

Christians are urged by society to leave their religion at home. But God tells them to go into all of society with the gospel message. This is real conferencing. You can never choose to leave your religion at home. Christians are required to carry the fullness of Christ's image to work. The image to be carried to the world is expressed in Isaiah 9:6.

For unto us a child is born, unto us a son is given: and the govern-
ment shall be upon his shoulder: and his name shall be called Won-
derful, Counseller, The mighty God, The everlasting Father, The
Prince of Peace.

The above Scripture verse is a summary of the Gospel Model. Christians can make Jesus' name wonderful by bringing the greatest Counselor of the ages to bear upon the awareness of society. Such an effort is the *Christian Assertive Effort.* Christian leaders in education must choose to do their work *as if unto God,* for Colossians 3:23 says, *And whatsoever ye do, do it heart-ily, as to the Lord, and not unto men.*

Christian laborers are required by God to teach from the Christian model rather than from a philosophical basis of hu-manism. The exclusion of God in the public schools, due to the public acceptance of humanism, makes the Christian task more difficult. It is a strange relationship that exists. The vast ma-jority of the public does not believe in a humanistic philosophi-cal position; yet, somehow the proponents of humanism have convinced the public that the rejection of God in public affairs is somehow the right thing to do. Christians must begin to con-fer the reason humanism is an incorrect tool for schools. Chris-tians must be conferencing this fact, time and time again, until the real point of view of the public is accepted.

Teaching from the Bible is not acceptable according to human-ism. However, it is possible to confer the Gospel Model in educa-tion by simply doing the model. The meaning of Christ's saying that we were to pick up the cross and follow Him is expressed in the doing. We must be like Shadrach, Meshach, and Abed-nego and give society the image of Christ whether it wants it or not. The followers of God would not give in and they would not perish in the fire. They would not go away. If the disciples of Christ had only gone to the parts of the world where they were welcomed, the

Gospel Model would not have spread from Jerusalem to societies around the world.

Christians must stand against humanism and they must state why! Most Christians would rather remain quiet than make trouble. But, the early disciples had the testimony that they tore up society with their teaching of Christ. In other words, wherever they went, their conferencing and manner of speaking created trouble in society for humanistic leaders of society. Christian's conferencing with others about Christ was the sword Jesus talked about, no doubt.

> . . . they drew Jason and certain brethren unto the rulers of the city, crying, These that have turned the world upside down are come hither also. (Acts 17:6)

How long has it been since someone was angry or nervous about your testimony for Christ? The point is that sometimes in achieving goals, one is required to speak and act boldly while speaking softly.

Counseling with the Gospel Model

Counseling is something people do that makes them feel good about themselves. To counsel another person can give the counselor a feeling of superiority in that they think they are experienced enough to tell somebody else what they should do. Professional counselors find this to be a problem when too many people think they can counsel another person. The truth is most people do not counsel others correctly and may do more harm than good. Professional counselors call this being harmfully involved. The major reason so many people who attempt to counsel others are harmfully involved is that they do not follow the rules of human behavior. There are many schools of behavior or many ways behavior can be viewed. Professional counselors are required to be familiar with the most respected schools of thought before they can obtain certification or license to counsel. Generally, a counselor will settle on one particular method of counseling with which to guide their counseling behavior. By giving advice and counsel to persons without knowledge of any of the schools of thought, you are viewed by the professional as a threat and danger to society.

Yet, nobody can really tell you not to counsel or to advise others even if they think you are harmfully involved. In fact, God tells us to confer or counsel others as part of sharing a complete gospel. To be like Christ requires one to be a counselor. A professional counselor follows one or more models of counseling. By learning how the Gospel Model explains behavior, means that the average citizen can give safe advice and counsel.

The counselor at school may ask permission to counsel your child. If the counselor's model comes from a humanistic school of thought, the counseling process will probably take the opposite view of the values you have been teaching your child. It is true that some counselors view religious beliefs as obstacles. Counselors are taught to be politically correct, which limits the counselor in the services provided.

What parents should be concerned about is whether or not the counselor is willing to use a model of behavior that aligns with absolute law found in the Constitution of the United States. This type of model will be the Gospel Model. To a Christian family, humanistic counseling is a terrible life event. We have already pointed out the weaknesses and flaws of humanistic models of behavior. The difference between a Christian and the professional is that Christians learn just one model, the Gospel Model, and follow it. Christians can become expert in counseling. There is only one way. The Gospel Model is to be used in every aspect of human existence.

You can be guided to counsel a person in a very helpful manner. This is not to be confused with treating emotionally ill persons, who need a trained therapist and doctor to treat them. The Gospel Model will help you to stay clear of being harmfully involved and not to conflict with the medical professions. The Gospel Model is excellent for everybody who is dealing with learned behaviors. Scout leaders, nurses, ministers, little league coaches, and friends need to know how to counsel via the Gospel Model.

In counseling, recall all the parts of the anatomy of the Gospel Model. Use your handbook to guide you in understanding the relationships that exist between mindsets, households, GOALS, SINS, heart, and mind. Until you have intellectually mastered the Gospel Model, your counseling may not be extremely effective. Work the model using the three-step approach. As you practice, your words will become more meaningful and helpful.

In Quick Success three excellent examples of Gospel Model counseling were examined. The main counseling was with parents. However, there was one particular child who was scheduled to enter Charter Ridge Hospital for a long stay and treatment. Joe's mother and I did some serious counseling with him.

Joe's mother was not his birth mother. Already, you know something was different in his learning as compared to normal children. Joe was abused badly before he learned to talk. His stomach was scared from cigarette burns. He had experienced starvation and seclusion from other children and adults. He became a child in the social service system and was adopted by his new mother. Joe was intelligent but did not have many social graces or academic skills. Joe was fortunate. His new mother was a Christian lady and believed it was God's will to have Joe as her son.

In the third grade, he was starved for attention. His behavior was so bad that he had to be separated from other children. Joe could not explain his behavior, neither could his teacher, his principal or his mother. He, however, was willing to do anything for attention. Joe brought only negative attention to himself.

One day Joe did a very bad thing before other children. That day I kept Joe in my office until his mother came to pick him up at school at which time my suggestion was to take Joe to Charter Ridge Hospital for an examination by a doctor. Joe's mother took him to Charter Ridge Hospital and he was to be admitted as soon as a room was available.

In the meantime Joe's mother and I used the Gospel Model of counseling with Joe. We had him to set goals in behavioral terms. Joe at first chose not to share all of these goals with us. Joe had been placed in special education and the learning disability class. His goal was to work himself out of that class. These classes did not enhance his self-image, which was very low. The three of us determined what had to be done, if Joe was to achieve his goals. His mother and I began with small goals for Joe, like sitting in his seat for fifteen minutes at a time. To fulfill his main goal, which at the end he shared with us, several similar goals had to be achieved. We not only helped Joe set goals but we continually praised and encouraged him that he could do these things. We did many normal and simple things for Joe and he ate up the attention. He was getting attention for doing positive things.

It is important that the counselor(s) have goals. Gospel Model counselors should always have the goal of changing SINS to GOALS. Knowing what the lifestyle of GOALS was like, we decided to build these characteristics in Joe's heart, representing new learning. Whereas Joe had automatically responded to school situations from a personality of SINS, it was a deliberate effort on our part to build a new heart in Joe's mind. Your handbook should tell you the difference between the heart and mind. Joe was not good at using his mind to explain his behavior, but he knew he was responding from unidentifiable urges coming from his heart. These unconscious urges were coming from the dark part of his heart created by the many terrible experiences he had as an infant. As Joe had said, he could not explain why he behaved the way he did, but he was willing to improve his behavior.

Joe knew he was under the control of something evil, making him respond in very unacceptable ways. Our counseling offered him hope that a change inside his heart could motivate him towards doing good things. What I learned was that secret evil thoughts, intents, and mindsets can be replaced by good mindsets. This type of psychological analysis is called *guided self-examination* in using the Gospel Model. Once a client understands the content of his heart, he can begin to replace darkness and evil responses can be replaced by good automatic responses.

At the end of the school year, Charter Ridge Hospital informed us that Joe did not need to be enrolled at Charter Ridge. They told us to keep up the good work and keep in touch. Joe spent the summer at the beach. When it was time to begin the new school year, he expressed his adopted goal to get out of special education classes. We re-evaluated Joe and were able to accommodate him. He struggled but kept up with his age group and class.

Joe has not become a doctor and will not be running for president. He did graduate from high school. He is married, has a child, and is working. These things were great miracles and accomplishments. Just to turn out rather normal was his miracle. Joe at some point in time began to deliberately train himself to respond to GOALS, which best explains his recovery. The Gospel Model of counseling has self-perpetuating powers of directing one's life. The Gospel Model did this great service for Joe.

Joe was a hard and difficult case. As a professional, I would come across maybe two or three children like Joe every five years. By that I mean we do not have the opportunity to serve seriously disturbed children very often. Most of the children in schools are normal children with normal problems. Joe can praise God that God had answered my prayer mentioned in chapter two. I really did know exactly what to say to Joe.

Most of the people you counsel will not have been as seriously affected as Joe. Shooting from the hip, however, will not work. Just thinking you know how to advise someone is selfish pride. Study and learn the Gospel Model of counseling, then you will be ready. Then you will be like Christ. Always use this formula with the three-step approach: B = E x G = Success.

Conflict and Stress Management

Professionals see the art of conflict management as a prerequisite for success. Companies, churches, educational institutions, government agencies, professional organizations, lawyers, doctors, executives and the armed forces spend millions of dollars each year on training to deal with conflict. These are continually looking for somebody to instruct them in how to manage conflict and stress.

In conflict management there is not a great pool of methods to learn from and it seems that previously used methods do not work or outlive their usefulness. The Gospel Model of conflict and stress management is different: it lasts forever and it works. Many scholars of conflict management focus on the conflict, the disagreement, the fight, or the anger generated by the conflict. The Gospel Model sees this as a great mistake.

True conflict management is more than containment; although when conflict has broken out, anger is released, then quieted. It is assumed that the conflict has been managed and the problem solved. This is grossly false. Containment is not management.

A perfect example of such management is found in my church denomination. Ministers are often appointed from one church to the next. The normal term of service is generally two years or less. The church has recognized this as a problem and believes that churches can have more continuity successes with pastors who remain at an appointment for many years. A ten-year term at a church guarantees the membership and community a better relationship.

What causes the need to exchange pastors so often and so soon? It is unresolved conflict, which is the cause of stress. To solve conflict between the membership and minister, the solution has been to move the minister to a new perish and provide a new minister for the unsatisfied perish. This usually works for a short time, until the old issues are renewed. There are many churches that go from one conference year to the next with the hope that a suitable minister will be named for their church. Instead of conflict management this is conflict perpetuation.

In such a scenario, the top hierarchy of the church is likely not to recognize the inefficiencies of the minister being reassigned. The hierarchy sees the conflict as unsolvable and appears to hope, if by chance, the ever-emerging conflict will go away with the exchange of personnel. They have forgotten that true Christians are peacemakers. The church hierarchy is prone to attribute failure to perpetual faults of the church's membership. With all of our seminaries, doctorates, and specialists, one would think that the church hierarchy would be able to better analyze the situation.

Who is at fault? The answer is simple. Every Christian in the hierarchy, every minister, and the membership of every local church that does not use the Gospel Model to manage conflict is at fault. If you do not use Christ in a complete gospel, you are at fault.

Everything starts from the top with Jesus Christ as the head of the church. Following God's example and model is the way to spiritual growth. Bishops should pass the word along to ministers to preach the Word of God and to use the Gospel Model. Properly done, the problem of revolving chairs in the ministry will end.

Revolving chairs is an endless covering of sins where the leadership of the church is unwilling to face the raging conflict. The Bible teaches clearly that sins must not be hidden and ignored, if progress is to occur: *He that covereth his sins shall not prosper: but whoso confesseth and forsaketh them shall have mercy* (Proverbs 28:13). Continually changing chairs is a symptom of the bureaucratic stress syndrome, which is prevalent in churches that do not have local autonomy. It is a church leadership pattern built around a Martha complex. Hierarchies tend to establish behaviors tied to busy work, bureaucratic clutter, and paper work. Like Martha, the leadership fails to choose the better part of worship and busies itself with mundane tasks. Not only does bureaucratic leadership choose Martha's worship style, it seeks out the spiritual Mary to attempt to convert her to worship like Martha. If Mary does not respond to Martha's demands, she is accused of not doing her part (Luke 10).

The Parable of the Bureaucrat Creating Stress

Generally, pastors who have been successful in their careers are elected to be superintendent. Having been appointed to such an office, a friend of mine discovered that his responsibilities had more than doubled. The clerical work overwhelmed him. His new job required that records of eighty churches had to be kept and evaluated. He had eighty ministers who answered to him, plus there were officers in the district who depended on his guidance. The new superintendent discovered that if he allocated the time to his ministers who needed counseling, there was not enough time to do the clerical work the district demanded.

As a pastor he had found ample time to counsel, visit, fellowship, do sermon preparation, and occasionally write articles for journals and other publications. Now he could not find time to write a newsletter to the district churches. He began to think the new job was too much for him and he began to have doubts and fears about his performance.

Experience could not guide him in his new leadership role, because he thought he had none. He began to demand more and more from his helpers and pastors. In turn, the pastors sensed his insecurities and apprehensions. Some suggested the new superintendent to be in over his head.

When he was a pastor, generally each new demand that came down from on high seemed to take away from his time to be pastor. Likewise, his pastors felt the same way about his new demands. As a pastor he had learned to gracefully ignore most of the demands from above. He spent his time in ministering within the Gospel Model. It was not obvious that he ignored his superintendent's demands because his church was a rapidly growing church, which made the superintendent look like a great leader. I reminded him that he had not really rebelled against his superintendent but had chosen to work within the Gospel Model rather than the Martha model. The Gospel Model had made him the most successful pastor in the district and me the most successful principal in the county school system, although both of us were still learning what this model really was.

Activity in his district slowed to a virtual stop. He realized the district was in decline under his leadership. He had asked for guidance from other superintendents and even from bishops. At this point in time, the whole denomination was in decline and he was receiving information from a pool of advisors who were not having success either, although they were more experienced.

When Superintendent Bruce Landreth had been my pastor, he taught me to pray and trust God. He watched over my development. As you know I was an at-risk child. He observed, as I quickly became a school principal. Seemingly, my success came effortlessly. New bigger assignments did not outgrow me. "What must I do to be successful," he asked me.

He was shocked to discover that my method of success was the one he had taught me. I simply had learned it better than he taught it. Next came the epiphany. What was the model for success outlined in the Bible? It was the Gospel Model of Jesus Christ. This was the only model that Christians are allowed to follow. My old pastor had forgotten this. He had successfully taught others to use the model of Christ but had failed to use it now in his new work.

Satan had overwhelmed him with menial tasks by convincing him that these chores had to be done and on time. He also believed that it was his responsibility to see to it that the ministers he supervised were successful. He had made plans to put pressure on the pastors in his district to be productive. He was following a model that was used by bureaucratic society where the men at the top demanded productivity from those below. This model works in the world or society and that was the reason Bruce and other superintendents were using this approach. He had been holding his pastors accountable just like his worldly model led him to do. However, both he and his pastors were not supposed to be of this society. Bruce was of the world and that was how he led the church

God wanted Bruce to examine himself to see if he was in the faith. When you feel lost, you may have taken your eyes off Christ and the way Christ does things. If you feel encumbered, it is likely that you have left the Gospel Model of behavior and have adopted the Martha model of behavior. What do you want to be? A successful leader as superintendent is what Bruce wanted. It was possible to enlarge Bruce's understanding of the Gospel Model at this time because as a Christian first, and a superintendent secondly, that was the model he wanted to follow. Bruce returned to his Gospel Model style of behavior. He began leadership of the district by teaching all his ministers to follow the Gospel Model. The district has been growing at a very quick pace. Many different programs initiated by the church received the credit for the new growth pattern but Bruce knew that Christ was the reason. The Gospel Model did not make Bruce the superintendent; it made him a better superintendent. He is now being considered for election as a bishop. If he is elected, he vows that all his superintendents will learn the Gospel Model of behavior.

In working with the Gospel Model, what must you do? Although Bruce continued to turn in reports on time, good record keeping did not make him a great superintendent. He assigned all record keeping to his secretary helper. Now, he was free to lead. Bruce immediately saw that being superintendent was not like being the head of a bureaucratic government. He began to rule over the house of God by serving and worshipping with his pastors.

Church government is different from secular government. In the Methodist Church we have the *Book of Discipline* as our guide. In content it is similar to many municipal governments. The difference is that the *Book of Discipline* was never intended to replace the leadership of the Holy Spirit in worship. Christ initiated a new type of worship, that of Spirit and truth. When the church worships in tune with Christ's direction, the *Book of Discipline* works fine. Once we acknowledge this truth, there will be an epiphany among us. Several changes will occur. Our government form will not change but it will be better.

How can it be better? We acknowledge that in membership the United Methodist Church is in decline. Could we be approaching the point of where God curses us for being unfruitful, as He did the fig tree? Since I have been a Methodist, many church-sponsored programs have come and gone. We are still in decline.

I am a fan of *The Purpose Driven Church* but the idea does not work everywhere or else the whole world would be turned upside down as it was when the Holy Spirit began the Gospel Model church on the day of Pentecost. *The Purpose Driven Church* has been successful in many places because God's Spirit has driven the concept towards success. The fact is that in the spiritual field of harvest, the timing required for success to occur is not the introduction of a new concept, such as *the Purpose Driven Church*, but the inclusion of *what and how* Christ told us to operate. Wherever the *Purpose Driven Church* has been successful, the model of Jesus Christ should be given the credit. In Christianity there is only one way. It really is important to believe that God adds to the church. It is really important to know we are working through the Gospel Model. This is our structure, this is our nourishment, and this water of life cannot be found elsewhere. He is the Bread, the Way, and the Model.

Ministering to a church, a school, or a large corporation has a common problem. None of these ever work well if conflict dominates the work place. In the Gospel Model of managing conflict, the factors of conflict are eliminated before a hostile breakout of dissatisfaction occurs. For example, the first meeting of the pastor with his church board must be designed to establish goals. If agreement is not possible here, there is no hope that the union will last for any length of time. In a church the main goals should be easy to agree upon. These goals are listed in most church manuals or books of discipline. Acceptance of goals cannot be left to previous times of acceptance. Things happen! Events occur that erode a church's commitments; the church leadership must keep the main goals and propositions before the membership by speaking often of the goals in agreement with the membership. The devil has an adequate supply of cares and stumbling blocks to diminish spiritual fervor and he will use these.

Once the church agrees what the main goals are, the listing of how the goals will be achieved is required. This listing of what has to happen for the church goals to be achieved may include job descriptions and programming. Allocation of responsibilities is reviewed and then assigned. New ideas can be presented. Whether something new should be tried is based on an explanation of how the new effort will accomplish the goals.

In the Gospel Model, conflict is resolved in the planning stages of God's work. The simple three-step approach will work if things are going to work. Ask the questions from the beginning. If Christians focus on the main goals, the church's ministers will have less conflicting issues with which to deal. It only takes disagreement to promote conflict. If agreement happens before conflict occurs, it may never occur. The secret is to keep planning, keep setting goals, keep being the church and keep bearing fruit. Godly thinking eliminates the bad effects of conflict.

The Christian, however, should never expect to be free of conflict and normally is the one to initiate conflict by asserting the message of God upon the world. But, never be part of sinful conflict, since certain behaviors are not to be named or used by the church or Christians (Ephesians 5:3). Nevertheless, righteous causes are very confrontational in turning society upside down. Be selective. Turning the world upside down brings stress mostly on society.

Sometimes in managing conflict the only choice is to stand. But stand quietly. You cannot avoid conflict if avoidance compromises the message of Christ. If you do not stand where God has placed you, those who persecute you will never recognize their evil doings. Once conflict has broken out in rage, the conflict is less manageable. Satan and SINS have taken control.

Confusion is of the devil and is his best weapon (1 Corinthians 14:33). Remember an important fact: hurt feelings, greed, and hate control the person overtaken by rage and spite. Conflict then makes the person the victim of stress and of SINS.

All those involved in conflict are victims of stress. The person who correctly manages the conflict will have less stress. Not even Jesus Christ was able to eliminate stress and still fulfill His purpose. To gain control, even during stressful episodes, it is important to use the Gospel Model with the three-step approach. What is your goal? How much humility are you willing to display? Most emotional tirades can be labeled as manic episodes and pass quickly. The person is out of control. The problem with quick release of stress and anger is that the person feels better after his emotional catharsis and assumes that feeling better is a spiritual assurance that the rage was justified. The Bible points this out to be the part of believing a lie (Romans 1:2).

On the other hand, your controlled response is difficult to manage by a raging person. Christ's peace entering the conflict can do much to solve an out-of-control emotional person. Always reply to manic behavior with soft words. It really does not matter too much what is said. It will be the tone of voice with which you say it that makes a difference. The goal is to turn away the wrath from the emotional scene so the peace of God can become part of the action. God's peace has understandings far beyond the moment of rage. Until the rage is over, do not expect to reason with out-of-control conflict (Proverbs 15:1).

If conflict is to be managed, the way one thinks must be altered. Confessions of bad behavior are crucial. Confess your faults, even if you think these faults have nothing to do with the conflict. You must be willing to be part of the responsibility for the human dilemma that involves SINS. Disagreement is not your style of living. If you do not already see that you are flawed, the other person in the conflict will be anxious to reveal this fact to you. Therefore, go ahead, confess your faults. This will help your opponent to admit his error. By doing this humble act, you may be saving the other person. This, I think, is the meaning of James 5:16.

> *Confess your faults one to another, and pray one for another, that ye may be healed. The effectual fervent prayer of a righteous man availeth much.*

Do you see who controls the conflict? God gives grace and wisdom to the humble and the repentant soul. When you have managed conflict like this, God is going to fill your heart with joy. When your enemy has come to his senses, he will thank you for being a light to him.

The best example that comes to mind is the conflict Job had with his tormentors, all of whom were sure that Job had committed great sins. Job was always willing to repent. He wanted his tormentors to show him his faults so he could confess them. Yet in the end, Job was judged by God to have been faithful. The tormentors saw things from a different model than Job's model. Job, although pained, managed his situation and conflicts. You can do this.

At-Risk Children

An underlying theme of this book has been focussed on children who are at risk. In the last ten years the term *at risk* has become part of the common language. We know what it means and all of society seems to unite to combat and understand at-risk factors in children. Children are our primary concern. With the Gospel Model, I have been able to practice a lifetime goal of reaching out to at-risk children. I have seen teachers, parents, and school administrators convert children who were termed at risk, into successfully orientated children and adolescents. It can be done.

As far as I am concerned, the explanation and use of the Gospel Model is the best chance we have to save children, to immunize them against failure, and to build a strong and adaptable lifestyle in children all the way through adulthood. You can help do this. As Dr. Larry said, "It may be your child." Who really knows what the Gospel Model can do when turned loose by a church or school on at-risk children? Go!

To order additional copies of

RAISING CHILDREN
THE BIBLE WAY
and the
CHRISTIAN
ASSERTIVE EFFORT

Have your credit card ready and call:

1-877-421-READ (7323)

or please visit our web site at
www.pleasantword.com

Also available at: www.amazon.com

Printed in the United States
92850LV00006BA/85-87/A

9 781414 100005